Jacques Pépin

Poulets & Légumes

Library of Congress Cataloging-in-Publication Data is available.
ISBN 978-0-544-92093-4 (hbk); 978-1-328-90072-2 (ebk)

Book design by Rachel Newborn

Printed in China
SCP 10 9 8 7 6 5 4 3 2 1

Jacques Pépin

Poulets & Légumes

My Favorite Chicken & Vegetable Recipes

A Rux Martin Book

HOUGHTON MIFFLIN HARCOURT

Boston • New York • 2018

Contents

POULETS · 7

LÉGUMES · 63

INDEX · 115

Poulets

Roast Chicken • 10

Roast Split Chicken with Mustard Crust • 13

Baked Chicken with Herb Crumbs • 14

Chicken with Cognac Sauce • 16

Peking-Style Chicken • 18

Spicy Chicken Breasts • 20

Chicken Breasts with Garlic and Parsley • 21

Chicken Breasts with Chervil Mousse • 22

Quick Coq au Vin • 24

Chicken African-Style with Couscous • 28

Chicken Diable • 30

Normandy Chicken Fricassee • 32

Chicken Mayonnaise • 34

Chicken Tonnato • 35

Chicken Suprêmes with Tapenade and Mushroom Sauce • 37

Chicken and Rice with Cumin and Cilantro • 39

Poulet à la Crème • 41

Crusty Chicken Thighs with Mushroom Sauce • 42

Chicken Bouillabaisse • 44

Chicken Chasseur • 46

Chicken Jardinière • 48

Chicken with Saffron
   Rice • 51

Sweet-and-Spicy Curried
   Chicken • 52

Grilled Chicken Tenders
   with Chimichurri • 54

Grilled Chicken with Tarragon
   Butter • 55

Grilled Chicken with Herb
   Sauce • 56

Basic Brown Sauce • 57

Grilled Chicken with Cabbage
   Anchoïade • 58

Roast Stuffed Cornish
   Hens • 60

ROAST CHICKEN

The classic way to cook chicken is still the simplest and best. Roasting the bird at high temperature crisps the skin as it protects the flesh, keeping it moist. And roasting the chicken on its side helps the legs, which usually take longer than the breast, cook faster, and also keeps the breast moist. Do not cover the bird with foil after it is roasted, or it will steam and taste reheated. For maximum flavor, the chicken should be served no more than 45 minutes after roasting.

1 chicken (about 3½ pounds)

½ teaspoon salt

½ teaspoon freshly ground
   black pepper

1 tablespoon olive oil

2–3 tablespoons water

1 bunch watercress, trimmed,
   washed, and dried

Preheat the oven to 425 degrees.

Sprinkle the chicken inside and out with the salt and pepper.

Heat the oil in a large ovenproof nonstick skillet until it is hot but not smoking. Place the chicken on its side in the skillet and brown it over medium-high heat for about 2½ minutes. Turn the chicken over and brown it on the other side for 2½ minutes.

Place the skillet, with the chicken still on its side, in the oven and roast, uncovered, for 20 minutes. Turn the chicken onto its other side and roast for another 20 minutes. Finally, turn the chicken onto its back, baste it with the fat that has emerged during cooking, and roast for 20 minutes, or until an instant-read thermometer reads between 150 and 160 degrees.

Remove the chicken from the oven and place it, breast side down to keep the breast meat moist, on a platter. Pour the drippings from the skillet into a bowl and set aside.

Deglaze the skillet by adding the water and stirring to loosen and melt the solidified juices. Add to the drippings in the bowl and let stand briefly, then skim off and discard most of the fat, leaving the natural pan juices.

To serve, carve the chicken, separating the drumsticks from the thighs and cutting each breast in half. Arrange a piece of dark meat and a piece of white meat on each of four plates. Garnish each serving with a few sprigs of watercress and serve with the pan juices.

ROAST SPLIT CHICKEN WITH MUSTARD CRUST

SERVES 4

I make this when I am in a hurry, because splitting and flattening the chicken and cutting between the joints of the leg and the shoulder reduce the cooking time by half. I pour the cooked chicken juices into a fat separator with a spout, leaving the fat behind.

MUSTARD CRUST

2 tablespoons chopped garlic

2 tablespoons Dijon mustard

2 tablespoons dry white wine

1 tablespoon soy sauce

2 tablespoons olive oil

1 teaspoon Tabasco sauce

1 teaspoon herbes de Provence

½ teaspoon salt

1 chicken (about 3½ pounds)

Fluffy Mashed Potatoes (page 101; optional)

Mustard Crust: Mix all the ingredients in a small bowl.

Preheat the oven to 450 degrees. Using kitchen shears or a sharp knife, cut alongside the backbone of the chicken to split it open. Spread and press on the chicken with your hands to flatten it. Using a sharp paring knife, cut halfway through both sides of the joints connecting the thighs and drumsticks and cut through the joints of the shoulder under the wings as well.

Put the chicken skin side down on a cutting board and spread it with about half the mustard mixture. Place the chicken flat in a large skillet, mustard side down. Spread the remaining mustard mixture on the skin side of the chicken. Cook over high heat for about 5 minutes, then place the skillet in the oven and cook the chicken for about 30 minutes. It should be well browned and dark on top.

Let the chicken rest in the skillet at room temperature for a few minutes, then cut it into 8 pieces with clean kitchen shears. Defat the cooking juices. If you like, mound some Fluffy Mashed Potatoes on each of four warm dinner plates and place 2 pieces of chicken on each plate. Pour some juice on the mashed potatoes and chicken and serve.

BAKED CHICKEN WITH HERB CRUMBS

Use fresh bread crumbs if possible for this dish. If you use dried crumbs, you'll need only half the amount called for.

The chicken can be prepared in advance to the point where it is marinated in the olive oil, Tabasco, and salt. The herb coating can also be prepared ahead, but don't put it on the bird until you are ready to cook it.

While the chicken is baking, sauté the liver briefly to serve with aperitifs, or enjoy it yourself while you are cooking.

1 chicken (about 3½ pounds)
1 tablespoon olive oil
½ teaspoon Tabasco sauce
¼ teaspoon salt

Preheat the oven to 425 degrees.

Cut the wing tips off the chicken. (The wing tips, neck, and gizzard can be frozen for use in stock or soup.) Using a sturdy knife or poultry shears and holding the chicken on its side, cut down along one side of the backbone. The backbone can be left on, but if you want to remove it, cut down along the other side of the bone to separate it. Spread the chicken open, lay it bone side down on the cutting board, and press it against the board with your hands to flatten it.

Pull off the skin; it should come off easily except, perhaps, around the wings. Remove as much skin as you can.

Place the chicken flesh side up on a large baking sheet and rub with the oil and Tabasco. Sprinkle with the salt.

HERB CRUMBS

- 2 fresh thyme sprigs or
  ½ teaspoon dried thyme

- 2 fresh oregano sprigs or
  ½ teaspoon dried oregano

- 3 slices firm white bread
  (3 ounces), processed to
  crumbs in a food processor
  (about 1½ cups)

- ¼ cup chopped fresh chives
  or parsley

- ½ teaspoon freshly ground
  black pepper

- 1 tablespoon olive oil

Herb Crumbs: If using fresh thyme and oregano, chop the leaves in a food processor or mini-chop or with a sharp knife. Combine the bread crumbs, thyme, oregano, chives or parsley, pepper, and oil in a bowl and toss gently to coat the bread crumbs lightly with the oil.

Pat the herb coating lightly over the surface of the chicken. Bake for 35 to 40 minutes, until the chicken is cooked through and the crumbs are nicely browned. Remove and let rest for 10 minutes.

Cut the chicken into pieces and serve. Discard the melted fat or use it to sauté potatoes.

CHICKEN WITH COGNAC SAUCE

SERVES 6 TO 8

The dish was the specialty of Le Pavillon restaurant, where I worked when I first came to New York City in 1959. In the old style, the chicken was carved in the dining room by the maître d'. Even for a single portion, a whole glorious chicken in a copper saucepan was brought to the guest's table. A rich sauce of chicken stock, cream, and cognac, enhanced by the glaze from the chicken juices, was served with it.

1 chicken (about 3½ pounds)

½ teaspoon salt

½ teaspoon freshly ground black pepper

1 tablespoon unsalted butter, softened

1 cup water

Preheat the oven to 425 degrees.

Sprinkle the chicken inside and out with the salt and pepper and rub all over with the butter. Place it on its side in a roasting pan and roast for 20 minutes. Turn onto the other side and roast for another 20 minutes. Turn the chicken breast side up and roast for 20 minutes. Transfer to a warm platter and set aside in a warm spot.

Discard all the fat that has accumulated in the pan. Deglaze the pan with the water, stirring to melt all the solidified juices, and pour the liquid through a fine strainer into a saucepan. Bring to a boil and reduce until as thick as syrup. (This is a poultry glaze; you should have about 1 tablespoon.) Transfer to a double boiler and keep warm.

Sauce: Combine the stock, wine, onion, and peppercorns in a medium heavy saucepan, bring to a boil, and boil to reduce by half.

Work the flour into the butter to make a beurre manié. Add it to the sauce, mixing constantly with a whisk, and simmer slowly for 3 minutes. Stir in the cream and reduce again

SAUCE

- 2 cups homemade chicken stock or low-sodium canned chicken broth
- ¾ cup dry white wine
- ½ cup chopped onion
- ½ teaspoon black peppercorns
- 1 tablespoon all-purpose flour
- 1 tablespoon unsalted butter, softened
- ½ cup heavy cream

  About 1½ teaspoons salt

  About ½ teaspoon freshly ground white pepper
- 2 tablespoons cognac

for 1 minute, or until the sauce reaches a nice smooth consistency and coats the spoon. Taste for seasoning and add salt and white pepper as needed (the amounts will depend on the seasoning of the chicken stock). Strain the sauce and stir in the cognac.

To serve, coat the chicken with the sauce, "sprinkle" the poultry glaze over the top, and serve. Alternatively, cut the bird into pieces and arrange on individual serving plates. Coat with the sauce, sprinkle with the poultry glaze, and serve.

PEKING-STYLE CHICKEN

Prepared in the style of Peking duck, the chicken is first blanched in boiling water to eliminate some of the fat and tighten the skin. This step helps the skin crisp as it cooks, so the bird becomes beautifully brown when it is roasted with a simple glaze of soy, honey, Tabasco, and vinegar.

1 chicken (about 4 pounds)

1½ teaspoons honey

2 tablespoons dark soy sauce

1 teaspoon Tabasco sauce

2 tablespoons balsamic vinegar

12 ounces small button mushrooms, cleaned

½ cup water

Preheat the oven to 375 degrees. Bring 10 cups water to a boil in a large pot.

Meanwhile, remove the wishbone from the chicken (see sidebar). Fold the wings of the chicken under its back and truss it with kitchen twine to help maintain the bird's compact shape (see sidebar).

Lower the chicken, breast side down, into the boiling water. Return the water to a boil over high heat (this will take about 3 minutes). As soon as the water is boiling, reduce the heat to low and simmer the chicken gently for 2 minutes. Drain and place the chicken breast side up on a rack in a roasting pan.

Mix the honey, soy sauce, Tabasco, and vinegar together in a small bowl. Brush the chicken on all sides with some of the mixture. Roast breast side up for about 30 minutes. Brush the breast side of the chicken again with the honey mixture, then roast for another 30 minutes.

Arrange the mushrooms in one layer under the rack in the pan and add the water. Brush the chicken with the remaining honey mixture and roast for 15 minutes longer.

Transfer the chicken to a platter. Pour the accumulated juices and the mushrooms into a saucepan. Let stand for 2 to 3 minutes, then spoon off as much fat from the surface as possible, and reheat if necessary.

Cut the chicken into pieces and serve with the juices and mushrooms.

♥ How to Remove the Wishbone from a Chicken

To remove the wishbone, place the bird on its back and lift the skin at the neck to expose the flesh. Slide the point of a paring knife along either side of the wishbone, cutting into the flesh (about ½ inch deep for a chicken). Then insert your thumb and index finger on either side of the wishbone and pry it out.

♥ How to Truss a Chicken

Trussing helps a bird hold its shape, whether it is stuffed or not, so it cooks evenly and looks better on the serving platter. Nevertheless, trussing is usually optional. To truss a chicken (or other bird), use fairly thick cotton kitchen twine, so it doesn't cut your fingers. Slide a length of twine under the tail and around the tips of the drumsticks, then cross the twine above the chicken and slide both ends of the twine under the tips of the drumsticks to create a figure 8. Hold the ends of the twine together, which will close the tail opening. Pull the ends of the twine around the sides of the bird until they join at the neck end, next to the wings, and tighten the twine, securing it behind the wings or behind the stump of the neck; tie a double knot so the twine doesn't slide off. Remove the twine before serving.

SPICY CHICKEN BREASTS

SERVES 4

This is a good make-ahead dish that is easy to prepare and very tasty. The spices for this rub are readily available in your supermarket spice rack, and the mix can be changed based on your taste preferences. Toasting the spices intensifies their flavor.

½ teaspoon juniper berries

½ teaspoon coriander seeds

½ teaspoon mustard seeds

½ teaspoon salt

4 boneless, skinless chicken breasts (about 6 ounces each)

1½ tablespoons olive oil

Combine the juniper berries, coriander seeds, and mustard seeds in a small skillet and cook over medium-high heat for 2 minutes, or until lightly toasted. Transfer the toasted spices to a spice grinder or coffee grinder, add the salt, and process for 20 to 30 seconds, until finely ground. Sprinkle both sides of the chicken breasts with the spice mixture and rub it gently into the meat. Brush the breasts on both sides with the oil. (The recipe can be prepared to this point up to 12 hours ahead. Wrap the chicken in plastic wrap and refrigerate until ready to cook.)

Preheat the oven to 180 degrees.

Heat a very large nonstick skillet until it is hot. Add the chicken breasts and cook over medium-high heat for 3 minutes. Turn the breasts over and cook for 3 minutes on the other side.

Arrange the breasts on an ovenproof platter and place them in the oven for at least 10 minutes to finish cooking. (The chicken can be kept warm in the oven for up to 45 minutes.)

Arrange a chicken breast on each of four dinner plates and serve.

CHICKEN BREASTS WITH GARLIC AND PARSLEY

SERVES 4

Cubes of chicken breasts are dredged in flour, sautéed over high heat in oil and butter, and finished with garlic and parsley and some fresh lemon juice. Make sure that you dry the cubes well with paper towels before you season them, and don't dredge them in the flour until just before sautéing. Finely milled Wondra flour will give you the crispest coating on the chicken; substitute all-purpose if you must. If possible, prepare this dish in a 12-inch skillet (preferably nonstick), which is large enough to accommodate the chicken in one layer.

3 boneless, skinless chicken breast halves (about 7 ounces each), cut into 1- to 1½-inch cubes

2 tablespoons Wondra flour

½ teaspoon salt

½ teaspoon freshly ground black pepper

2 tablespoons good olive oil

1 tablespoon chopped garlic

3 tablespoons chopped fresh parsley

2 tablespoons unsalted butter

1 lemon, quartered

Dry the chicken cubes with paper towels and toss them with the flour, salt, and pepper in a bowl. Heat the oil in a 12-inch skillet over high heat until very hot but not smoking, add the chicken cubes, and cook in one layer, turning occasionally, for about 3½ minutes. Meanwhile, combine the garlic and parsley in a small bowl. Add the butter and the parsley mixture to the skillet and sauté for 1 minute longer, shaking the skillet occasionally to coat the chicken.

To serve, divide among four plates, add a wedge of lemon to each plate, and serve within 15 minutes.

CHICKEN BREASTS WITH CHERVIL MOUSSE

SERVES 6

The mousse for this special dish can be flavored with other types of herbs, mushrooms, or different spices. Instead of the cognac sauce, the stuffed chicken breasts can be served with the pan drippings only.

You may have to order the skin-on boneless breasts ahead.

MOUSSE

- 1 pound boneless, skinless chicken thighs, cut into chunks
- ¼ cup chopped ice
- 1 cup loosely packed fresh chervil or tarragon leaves
- 1 cup very cold heavy cream
- 1 teaspoon salt
- ¼ teaspoon freshly ground black pepper

- 6 skin-on boneless chicken breasts
- ¼ teaspoon salt
- 2 tablespoons unsalted butter
- ⅓ cup water

Mousse: Put the chicken, ice, and chervil or tarragon in a food processor and process for about 10 seconds. Scrape down the sides with a rubber spatula and process for 10 seconds more.

Clean the sides of the bowl again and process for another 10 seconds. With the motor running, add the cream in a slow stream, then add the salt and pepper and process briefly to mix. Transfer to a bowl. (The mousse can be made several hours ahead and refrigerated until ready to use.)

To stuff the chicken breasts: Remove the fillet (tender) from each breast and remove and discard the sinew from each one. Set aside the fillets.

Place the chicken breasts skin side up on the work surface. Pull back the skin and spoon about ½ cup of the mousse on top of the meat. Arrange a fillet on one side of each breast, pressing it into the mousse, then bring the skin back over the mousse so it covers the whole surface.

Hold a stuffed breast skin side down in the palm of one hand and bring the edges of the skin around to the underside of the breast; the skin will not come all around the breast. Repeat with the remaining breasts. (The breasts can be

SAUCE

- 1 cup homemade chicken stock or low-salt canned chicken broth
- ½ cup dry white wine
- ½ cup heavy cream
- 1 teaspoon potato starch dissolved in 1 tablespoon water
- 1 tablespoon cognac
- ¼ teaspoon salt
- ¼ teaspoon freshly ground black pepper

stuffed several hours ahead; arrange skin side down on a tray and refrigerate, covered.)

At serving time, sprinkle the chicken breasts with the salt. Heat 1 tablespoon of the butter in each of two skillets, preferably nonstick. When it is hot, add the chicken skin side down and sauté over high heat for about 4 minutes. Cover, reduce the heat, and cook gently for 10 minutes. (The chicken is cooked only on the skin side so the meat won't toughen.)

Remove the lid and continue cooking until the juices are reduced and the chicken is sizzling in the fat and nicely browned. Remove to a serving platter and set aside in a warm place.

There will be a lot of fat in the pan drippings because of the skin. Boil down the drippings until the juices caramelize into a glaze on the bottom of the skillet and the clear fat is on top. Let sit for 1 to 2 minutes, then pour off most of the fat and discard. Add the water to the skillet and bring to a boil, then strain through a sieve into a small saucepan. Reduce again until you have about 3 tablespoons concentrated juices, or glaze.

Meanwhile, for the sauce: Bring the chicken stock and wine to a boil in a medium saucepan and boil to reduce to 1 cup. Add the cream and bring to a boil again, then add the dissolved potato starch. Add the cognac, salt, and pepper and strain through a fine sieve.

Pour the sauce over the chicken breasts, sprinkle with the chicken glaze, and serve.

QUICK COQ AU VIN

Traditionally, coq au vin, or chicken with red wine, had to be cooked for a long time because the coq *("cock"—an older chicken) was tough. Now the dish can be made quickly with tender parts either cut from a young chicken or bought separately at the market. I divide the chicken into pieces, remove the skin, brown it, and cook it in the red wine, adding the breasts at the end so they don't get overdone. I glaze the onions separately in a little olive oil and sugar, stirring the mushrooms in near the end. Finally, I combine everything and serve it with large heart-shaped croutons.*

1 chicken (3½–4 pounds) or 2 whole boneless chicken legs plus 2 whole boneless, skinless breasts

12 small pearl onions (6 ounces)

2 tablespoons olive oil

½ teaspoon sugar

½ cup water

4 large mushrooms (4 ounces), cleaned and quartered

⅓ cup finely chopped onion

3 garlic cloves, crushed and finely chopped (2 teaspoons)

1½ cups fruity, dry, robust red wine (such as Syrah or Grenache)

1 fresh thyme sprig or ½ teaspoon dried thyme

If using a whole chicken, cut off the wings and cut them at the joints into 3 pieces each. Cut the chicken into 4 pieces: 2 breasts and 2 legs. Skin and bone the breasts. Set the breasts aside with the 4 meatier wing pieces. (Freeze the bones and wing tips for stock, if desired.)

To bone the chicken legs, first pull off the skin and cut the tips off the drumsticks. Then cut down each side of the thighbone and slide your knife under the bone to separate the meat from it. Holding the thighbone, cut all around the joint at the knee to loosen the meat. Scrape down the drumstick bone and pull out the bones. Set the legs aside with the breasts and wing pieces.

Put the pearl onions, 1 tablespoon of the olive oil, the sugar, and the water in a large saucepan, bring to a boil over high heat, and boil until the water has evaporated and the onions start frying. Continue to cook, stirring or shaking the pan occasionally, until the onions are glazed on all sides. Add the mushrooms and sauté for 1 minute. Set aside, covered.

2 bay leaves

¾ teaspoon salt

¾ teaspoon freshly ground
black pepper

1 teaspoon potato starch
dissolved in 2 tablespoons
red wine

CROUTONS

4 slices firm white bread
(4 ounces)

2 teaspoons canola oil

2 tablespoons finely chopped
fresh parsley

Preheat the oven to 400 degrees.

Heat the remaining 1 tablespoon oil in a large skillet. When it is hot, add the chicken wing pieces, if you have them, and sauté for 2 to 3 minutes, until lightly browned on all sides. Add the legs and brown for 2 to 3 minutes on each side. Add the breasts and brown for 2 minutes on each side. Remove all the chicken pieces to a plate.

Add the chopped onion to the drippings in the skillet and sauté for 1 minute. Add the garlic and cook for about 10 seconds. Add the wine, thyme, bay leaves, salt, and pepper and bring to a boil. Return the legs and the wings to the pan, cover, and boil very gently for 5 minutes. Add the chicken breasts and boil gently for another 6 minutes.

Add the dissolved potato starch to the chicken and stir until the pan juices are thickened. Add the pearl onions and mushrooms, with their juices. Keep warm.

continued

Croutons: Meanwhile, trim the crusts from the bread and cut each slice diagonally in half to form 2 triangles. Trim each triangle into a heart-shaped crouton.

Spread the canola oil on a cookie sheet and press the croutons into the oil so they are moistened on both sides. Bake for 8 to 10 minutes, until nicely browned.

At serving time, dip the tip of each crouton into the sauce to moisten it and then into the chopped parsley. Cut the chicken breast pieces and legs in half. Serve 1 breast piece, 1 drumstick or thigh, and, if you have them, 1 piece of wing per person, with 2 croutons, along with some of the sauce and vegetables. Sprinkle the remaining chopped parsley over the chicken.

CHICKEN AFRICAN-STYLE WITH COUSCOUS

I learned this recipe from my brother, who lived in Senegal for several years. There it is usually served with "broken rice," which are grains of rice broken into bits; when cooked, they look a bit like the couscous that I use here. Marinating the chicken in lime juice, ginger, garlic, and hot pepper flakes gives it a robust and distinctive taste.

MARINADE

- 2 cups very thinly sliced onion
- 4–6 garlic cloves, crushed and finely chopped (1½ tablespoons)
- ½ teaspoon hot pepper flakes
- 1½ teaspoons grated ginger
- 1 teaspoon salt
- ¼ teaspoon freshly ground black pepper
- ¼ cup fresh lime juice

- 1 chicken (3½–4 pounds), cut into 8 pieces (2 legs, 2 thighs, and 2 breasts, halved)

Marinade: Mix all the ingredients together in a large bowl.

Add the chicken pieces to the marinade and turn to coat. Cover and refrigerate for 4 to 5 hours, or as long as overnight.

Cut off the little bits of fat clinging to the chicken thighs and cut the fat into small pieces.

Melt the fat in a large saucepan. Add the chicken pieces (set the marinade aside) and brown them in the fat, about 10 minutes. Transfer the chicken to a medium stainless steel pot.

Deglaze the saucepan with the marinade, stirring to melt the solidified juices, and add to the chicken. Bring to a boil, cover, reduce the heat, and simmer slowly for 25 minutes. Remove the cover and boil over high heat for 5 minutes to reduce the sauce.

COUSCOUS

2 tablespoons unsalted butter

2 cups instant couscous

1¾ cups boiling water

¼ teaspoon salt

Couscous: Meanwhile, melt the butter in a saucepan. Add the couscous and mix carefully so that all the grains are coated with butter. Pour the boiling water over the grains, add the salt, cover, and let stand for 10 minutes, off the heat. Stir with a fork to separate the grains.

Mound the couscous on a serving platter, arrange the chicken around it, and serve.

CHICKEN DIABLE

For a special family meal, serve this chicken and a simple salad with a vinegar-and-oil dressing. For a slightly less pungent sauce for the bird, substitute white wine for half the vinegar.

1 chicken (3½–4 pounds), or 2 whole chicken legs, drumsticks and thighs separated, plus 2 boneless, skinless breasts

¾ teaspoon salt

¾ teaspoon coarsely ground black pepper

1 tablespoon oil

1 tablespoon unsalted butter

4 garlic cloves, crushed and finely chopped (about 1 tablespoon)

¼ cup red wine vinegar

¼ cup water

¾ cup tomato puree or sauce

1 teaspoon Tabasco sauce

1 tablespoon chopped fresh tarragon or 2 tablespoons coarsely minced fresh parsley

If using a whole chicken, cut off the chicken legs at the joint. If desired, chop off the tips of the drumsticks (reserve for stock). Separate the drumsticks from the thighs. Cut off the wings, leaving the first joints attached to the breasts (reserve the wings for stock). Remove the wishbone by cutting along each side of it and pulling it out. Remove the 2 breasts, cutting them off at the shoulder and down each side of the breastbone; the breasts will be boneless except for the first joint of the wings. Pull off all the chicken skin and discard it.

If using chicken parts, pull the skin off the drumsticks and thighs and discard.

Sprinkle the chicken with ½ teaspoon salt and ½ teaspoon pepper.

Heat the oil and butter in a large heavy skillet until hot. Add the drumsticks and thighs, cover, and sauté over medium-high heat for 5 minutes. Turn the pieces over and cook, covered, for 3 more minutes. Add the breasts skinned side down, cover, and cook for about 8 more minutes, until nicely browned. Transfer the chicken pieces to a serving platter and set aside in a warm place.

Add the garlic to the drippings in the pan and cook, stirring, for 20 to 30 seconds, without browning it. Deglaze the pan with the vinegar, stirring to melt all the solidified juices, and cook for 1 to 2 minutes; most of the vinegar should have evaporated. Add the water and tomato puree or sauce, bring to a boil, cover, and boil over high heat for 1 minute. Stir in the remaining ¼ teaspoon salt and ¼ teaspoon pepper, and the Tabasco.

Spoon the sauce over the chicken, garnish with the tarragon or parsley, and serve.

NORMANDY CHICKEN FRICASSEE

SERVES 4

Chicken in cream and wine sauce with a vegetable garnish is often featured in the restaurants of Normandy. It is always flavored with Calvados (apple brandy).

- 1 chicken (about 3½ pounds), cut into 8 pieces (2 legs, 2 thighs, and 2 breasts, halved), skin removed
- ½ teaspoon salt, or to taste
- ½ teaspoon freshly ground black pepper, or to taste
- 3 tablespoons unsalted butter
- 1 cup diced (½-inch) carrots
- 1½ cups diced (1-inch) onion
- ½ cup diced (½-inch) celery
- 2 garlic cloves, coarsely chopped (1 teaspoon)
- 2 tablespoons chopped fresh parsley
- ¼ teaspoon dried thyme
- 1 bay leaf
- 1 cup dry white wine (such as Chardonnay)

Sprinkle the chicken pieces with the salt and pepper.

Heat 2 tablespoons of the butter in a large heavy nonstick skillet. When it is hot, add the chicken pieces, reduce the heat to medium, and cook for 5 minutes, turning the pieces once or twice.

Add the carrots, onions, celery, garlic, parsley, thyme, and bay leaf, cover, and cook for 5 minutes. Add the wine and water, bring to a simmer, cover, and simmer for about 20 minutes, or until the chicken is tender when pierced with a fork.

Meanwhile, blend the remaining 1 tablespoon butter with the flour to make a beurre manié. Lift the cooked chicken from the pan and arrange on a serving platter; set aside in a warm place.

½ cup water

1 tablespoon all-purpose flour

½ cup heavy cream

½ cup frozen baby peas

2 tablespoons Calvados or
applejack

Add the beurre manié to the sauce, whisking steadily. Add the cream and peas and bring to a boil, then reduce the heat and simmer for 1 minute. Remove from the heat, stir in the Calvados or applejack, and taste for seasoning; add salt and pepper if needed.

Pour the sauce over the chicken and serve.

CHICKEN MAYONNAISE

This is a great dish to serve on a hot summer day for a lunch or to feature on a buffet. The chicken can be cooked up to a day ahead and refrigerated. Then bring the beautifully assembled dish to the table or buffet to serve.

1 chicken (3½–4 pounds)

1 medium carrot, peeled

1 medium onion

4 whole cloves

1 teaspoon salt

½ teaspoon freshly ground black pepper

8 cups water

1 large head Boston lettuce

1 cup mayonnaise

1 tablespoon Dijon mustard

2 hard-cooked eggs, quartered

2 ripe tomatoes, cut into 4 wedges each

1 2-ounce can anchovy fillets in oil

2 tablespoons well-drained capers

5–6 fresh parsley sprigs, leaves removed and chopped

Put the chicken in a stockpot and add the carrot, onion, cloves, salt, pepper, and water. Bring to a simmer and simmer for 30 minutes.

Cool the chicken in the broth for at least 30 minutes. (The chicken can be cooked up to a day ahead; transfer to a platter and refrigerate. If desired, strain the stock and reserve for another use.)

Pull off the outer leaves from the head of lettuce, leaving the center heart (about 2 inches long) intact. Wash and dry the lettuce leaves and cut crosswise into ½-inch-wide strips.

Skin the chicken and pull the meat off the bones in large pieces, then cut into thin slices.

Mix the mayonnaise with the mustard.

Put the shredded lettuce in a large glass bowl. Arrange the sliced chicken on top of the lettuce and coat with the mayonnaise, spreading it with a spatula so that all the chicken is coated. Stand the lettuce heart in the center of the mayonnaise (you may have to push the pieces of chicken aside to make a hole so that the heart can stand up) and arrange the quartered eggs, tomatoes, anchovy fillets, and capers in an attractive pattern on top. Sprinkle with the chopped parsley and serve.

CHICKEN TONNATO

Inspired by the famous Italian dish vitello tonnato *(veal in tuna sauce), my chicken tonnato is made with skinless, boneless breasts poached in a vegetable broth and served on a bed of arugula. The sauce is made in seconds in a food processor. Canned tuna (preferably in oil) is the main ingredient in the sauce, which also includes anchovies, mustard, and lemon juice. The delicious poaching broth is served as a soup accompaniment. Any leftover chicken tonnato makes a great sandwich.*

CHICKEN

½ cup sliced onion

½ cup sliced leek, washed well

1 cup sliced white button mushrooms

½ cup diced (½-inch) carrot

½ cup diced (½-inch) celery

1 teaspoon salt

¼ teaspoon freshly ground black pepper

5 cups water

4 boneless, skinless chicken breast halves (about 6 ounces each)

continued

Chicken: Combine the onion, leek, mushrooms, carrot, celery, salt, pepper, and water in a large saucepan (preferably stainless steel). Bring to a boil, reduce the heat to medium-low, and boil gently for 5 minutes. Add the chicken breasts and cook them just until the broth returns to a boil, about 4 minutes. Boil for about 15 seconds, then remove the pan from the heat, cover, and let the breasts stand in the broth for 12 to 15 minutes.

Tuna Sauce: Meanwhile, set aside 4 of the anchovies for the garnish. Put the tuna and the remaining anchovies in a food processor, along with the oil from both of the cans. Add the egg yolk, mustard, lemon juice, water, salt, and Tabasco and process for a few seconds. With the processor running, add the olive oil in a slow stream and process for a few seconds, or until it is well incorporated and the sauce is smooth.

TUNA SAUCE

- 1 (2-ounce) can anchovy fillets in oil
- 1 (3-ounce) can tuna (preferably in oil)
- 1 large egg yolk
- 1 tablespoon Dijon-style mustard
- 1 tablespoon fresh lemon juice
- 1 tablespoon water
- ¼ teaspoon salt
- ¼ teaspoon Tabasco sauce
- ½ cup extra-virgin olive oil

- 4 cups (loosely packed) arugula leaves, washed and dried
- 1 tablespoon drained capers
- 1 tablespoon minced fresh chives

At serving time, divide the arugula among four plates. Remove the chicken breasts from the broth with a slotted spoon. Cut each breast into 4 crosswise slices, and arrange the slices on top of the arugula. Generously coat the chicken with the tuna sauce and top each serving with 1 of the reserved anchovy fillets. Sprinkle on some capers and chives and serve at room temperature. Reheat the broth, divide among four bowls, and serve with the chicken.

CHICKEN SUPRÊMES WITH TAPENADE AND MUSHROOM SAUCE

Boneless, skinless chicken breasts are called suprêmes. Some markets offer organic or free-range chicken, which is my choice for this recipe. Tapenade is a Provençal mixture of olives, capers, and anchovy fillets. To mine I add a little garlic and some apricots for a bit of zing and sweetness. While tapenade is excellent served on toast or baguette slices with aperitifs, it is used here as a stuffing for chicken breasts. The breasts can be stuffed ahead and sautéed at the last moment.

I often use wild mushrooms for the sauce in summer because hunting for mushrooms in the woods is one of my greatest pleasures. Baby bellas, creminis, or regular white ones are perfectly fine, though, for this dish.

TAPENADE

- ¾ cup mixed pitted black oil-cured, kalamata, and green olives
- 1 small garlic clove, sliced
- 2 dried apricot halves, cut into small pieces
- 1½ tablespoons drained capers
- 8 anchovy fillets in oil
- 2 tablespoons extra-virgin olive oil

continued

Tapenade: Put all the ingredients in a food processor and pulse to make a coarse puree.

Cut a horizontal slit in each chicken breast to create a pocket and stuff with the tapenade.

When ready to cook the chicken, preheat the oven to 180 degrees. Heat the oil and 2 tablespoons of the butter in a large skillet. Meanwhile, season the stuffed chicken breasts with ½ teaspoon each salt and pepper and arrange them side by side in the hot skillet. Cook over medium heat, covered, for about 3 minutes on each side. Transfer to a platter. Keep warm in the oven.

Add the mushrooms and onion to the skillet and sauté for about 2 minutes. Add the wine and reduce by boiling for 2 minutes. Add the remaining 2 tablespoons butter and salt and pepper to taste and mix well to incorporate the butter.

- 4 boneless, skinless chicken breasts (about 6 ounces each)
- 1 tablespoon good olive oil
- 4 tablespoons (½ stick) unsalted butter

  Salt and freshly ground black pepper, to taste
- 1½ cups washed and diced (¾-inch) baby bella mushrooms
- ½ cup chopped onion
- ½ cup dry white wine
- 2 tablespoons chopped fresh chives or parsley, for garnish

Serve a chicken breast on each of four hot plates. Add any juice that has accumulated around them on the platter to the mushroom sauce in the pan. Spoon the mushrooms and sauce over the chicken breasts and sprinkle the chives or parsley on top. Serve.

CHICKEN AND RICE WITH CUMIN AND CILANTRO

SERVES 6 TO 8

Chicken with rice, or arroz con pollo, *is a staple at our house. This dish is highly seasoned with cumin, ginger, garlic, and a great deal of cilantro. We like it best when it is made with chicken wings. If you buy whole wings, remove the tips and save them for stock; cut the remaining sections apart so you have two meaty pieces. In my market, I can usually buy my wings already trimmed.*

2 tablespoons olive oil

3 pounds chicken wings (about 20), tips (if any) removed, remaining sections separated into 2 pieces each

2½ cups coarsely chopped onion

¼ cup coarsely chopped garlic

¼ cup coarsely chopped peeled ginger

2 cups (about 13 ounces) Carolina long-grain white rice

1½ tablespoons ground cumin

1 (14½-ounce) can diced tomatoes

2½ teaspoons salt

1 tablespoon Sriracha or other hot chili sauce

2½ cups water

1½ cups chopped fresh cilantro stems, plus ½ cup chopped, for garnish (optional)

Heat the olive oil in a 12- to 14-inch skillet or a pot large enough to hold the chicken wings in one layer. Dry the wings with paper towels, place them in the hot oil, and brown over high heat, uncovered, for about 8 minutes. Turn the wings over with tongs and brown them on the other side for 8 minutes. Using the tongs, transfer the browned wings to a bowl.

Add the onions, garlic, and ginger to the drippings in the skillet and cook for 2 to 3 minutes. Add the rice and cumin and mix well, then add the tomatoes, salt, sriracha, water, and chopped cilantro stems and mix well.

Return the wings to the pan and bring to a strong boil. Cover, reduce the heat to low, and cook for about 30 minutes, or until the wings are cooked through.

Serve the stew garnished with the chopped cilantro, if desired.

POULET À LA CRÈME

Chicken in cream sauce is a specialty of the town where I was born, Bourg-en-Bresse. My mother's simple recipe included a whole cut-up chicken with water, a pinch of flour, and a bit of cream to finish. I have added white wine and mushrooms to make the dish a bit more sophisticated, and used chicken thighs, which are the best part of the chicken (1½ thighs per person should be a generous serving for a main course). A sprinkling of chopped tarragon at the end makes it more special, but it is optional. Most of the time, my mother served hers with rice pilaf.

2 tablespoons unsalted butter

6 chicken thighs (about 3 pounds), skin removed (about 2½ pounds skinned)

8 mushrooms (about 6 ounces), cleaned and sliced

1½ tablespoons all-purpose flour

½ cup dry white wine

¼ cup water

¾ teaspoon salt

¾ teaspoon freshly ground black pepper

½ cup heavy cream

1 tablespoon coarsely chopped fresh tarragon (optional)

Melt the butter in a large saucepan. Add the chicken thighs to the pan in one layer and brown over high heat for about 2½ minutes on each side.

Add the mushrooms to the pan and sprinkle on the flour. Turn the chicken pieces with tongs so the flour is dispersed evenly. Stir in the wine and water and mix well. Bring to a boil and add the salt and pepper. Cover, reduce the heat, and cook gently for 25 minutes.

Add the cream, bring to a boil, and boil, uncovered, for about 1 minute.

Serve sprinkled with the chopped tarragon, if desired.

CRUSTY CHICKEN THIGHS WITH MUSHROOM SAUCE

I cook the thighs in a skillet skin side down here, so the skin becomes crisp, dry, and beautifully browned. Make sure to use a nonstick skillet with a tight-fitting lid, so as the skin fries, the flesh is cooked by the steam. The portions are relatively small here, but within the context of a menu this is enough meat.

4 large chicken thighs (about 1¾ pounds total), skin on

¾ teaspoon salt

¾ teaspoon freshly ground black pepper

1 cup diced (¼-inch) onion

1½ tablespoons coarsely chopped garlic

3 cups washed and diced (½-inch) baby bella or white mushrooms

⅓ cup dry white wine

1 tablespoon chopped fresh chives, for garnish

Arrange the chicken thighs skin side down on a cutting board. Using a sharp paring knife, trim off any excess skin at the edges and cut about ½ inch deep into the flesh on either side of the thigh bone. (This will help the meat cook more quickly.) Sprinkle the thighs with ½ teaspoon each of the salt and pepper and arrange them skin side down in one layer in a nonstick skillet with a tight-fitting lid.

Place the skillet over high heat, and when the thighs start sizzling, reduce the heat to medium, cover tightly, and cook for 16 to 18 minutes, checking occasionally to make sure the chicken is browning properly. Meanwhile, preheat the oven to 150 degrees. If the chicken seems to be cooking too fast after 10 minutes or so, reduce the heat to low. The skin of the chicken should be very crisp and brown. Transfer the chicken skin side up to an ovenproof platter and place it in the oven.

Discard all but 2 tablespoons fat from the skillet in which you cooked the chicken. Add the onion, garlic, and mushrooms and sauté them over high heat for about 3 minutes.

Sprinkle the remaining ¼ teaspoon salt and ¼ teaspoon pepper on the mushrooms and then add the wine and any liquid that has accumulated around the thighs on the platter. Cook the sauce over high heat for about 1 minute to reduce the liquid.

To serve, divide the sauce among four hot plates. Place a thigh in the middle of the mushroom sauce on each plate, spoon some sauce over, sprinkle on the chives, and serve.

CHICKEN BOUILLABAISSE

This dish, made with chicken, kielbasa, and potatoes, takes its inspiration from the famous fish stew of the south of France and contains all the classic seasonings, including saffron. An expensive spice, saffron is essential to this dish. The best comes from Spain. I've also added a little tarragon at the end. Although not absolutely necessary, tarragon has a slight anise taste that complements the other seasonings. To reinforce its flavor, I add a splash of Pernod or Ricard at the last minute, although this ingredient is optional too. I serve my chicken bouillabaisse with a traditional rouille, a garlicky mayonnaise seasoned with cayenne and paprika.

Yes, there are lots of ingredients in this recipe, but it's quick to assemble and cooks in about 30 minutes. It makes a meal in itself when followed by a salad and some cheeses.

BOUILLABAISSE

- 1 tablespoon good olive oil
- 1 tablespoon coarsely chopped garlic
- ½ teaspoon saffron threads
- 1 teaspoon grated lemon rind
- ¾ teaspoon salt
- ½ teaspoon freshly ground black pepper
- ¼ teaspoon fennel seeds
- ¼ teaspoon herbes de Provence
- ½ cup coarsely chopped onion
- ¼ cup coarsely chopped celery

Bouillabaisse: Mix the oil, garlic, saffron, lemon rind, salt, pepper, fennel seeds, herbes de Provence, onion, celery, and carrot in a large bowl. Add the chicken thighs and turn to coat. Cover and refrigerate until you are ready to cook.

Transfer the contents of the bowl to a stainless steel pot and add the tomatoes, wine, water, and potatoes. Cover, bring to a boil over high heat, then reduce the heat to low and boil gently for 25 minutes. Add the sausage and cook for 5 minutes longer. If adding Pernod or Ricard, stir it in now with the tarragon.

Rouille: Remove half a cooked potato and ¼ cup liquid from the pot and place in a food processor with the garlic, cayenne, and paprika. Process for 10 seconds. Add the egg

continued

¼ cup coarsely chopped carrot

4 chicken thighs (about 1¾ pounds total), skin and fat removed

½ (14½-ounce) can diced tomatoes (about 1 cup)

½ cup dry white wine

¾ cup water

5 red or Yukon Gold potatoes (about 12 ounces total), peeled and halved

1 piece (about 10 ounces) kielbasa sausage, cut into 4 pieces

2 teaspoons Pernod or Ricard (optional)

1 tablespoon chopped fresh tarragon, chives, or parsley

ROUILLE

2 large garlic cloves

⅛ teaspoon cayenne pepper

¼ teaspoon paprika

1 large egg yolk

½ cup good olive oil

Salt, to taste

yolk. With the processor running, slowly add the oil until it is incorporated. Taste for salt and adjust, if needed.

Serve the bouillabaisse in warmed soup plates with a spoonful of the rouille drizzled on top.

CHICKEN CHASSEUR

Chasseur *means "hunter" in French, and the term refers to a poultry or meat dish with mushrooms, tomato, and garlic; it is similar to an Italian cacciatore. My update of the classic French stew uses skinless chicken thighs in place of chicken pieces with skin. After sautéing the thighs in a little olive oil, I finish them in a sauce containing onion and leek, flavoring it in the traditional manner.*

The dish can be prepared up to a day ahead. At serving time, reheat it gently.

2 tablespoons olive oil

8 chicken thighs (about 3 pounds), skin removed

1 small leek, trimmed (leaving some green), split, washed, and coarsely chopped (1¾ cups)

1 cup chopped onion

1½ tablespoons all-purpose flour

1 cup dry white wine

1 (15-ounce) can whole tomatoes in juice

5–6 garlic cloves, crushed and finely chopped (1½ tablespoons)

20 medium mushrooms (about 12 ounces), cleaned

1 teaspoon chopped fresh thyme

Heat the oil in a large deep nonstick skillet until hot. Add the chicken thighs in one layer and cook over medium-high heat for 3 minutes on each side, or until lightly browned. Transfer to a plate.

Add the leek and onion to the drippings in the skillet and sauté for 30 seconds. Add the flour, mix it in well, and cook for about 30 seconds. Mix in the wine and tomatoes and bring to a boil over medium heat.

Add the chicken thighs, garlic, mushrooms, thyme, rosemary, salt, pepper, and soy sauce and bring to a boil over high heat, stirring occasionally to prevent scorching. Cover the pan, reduce the heat to low, and cook for about 20 minutes. Sprinkle on the chervil or tarragon and mix it in.

1 teaspoon chopped fresh
   rosemary

¾ teaspoon salt

½ teaspoon freshly ground
   black pepper

1 tablespoon dark soy sauce

1 tablespoon chopped fresh
   chervil or tarragon

Serve 2 thighs per person, with some of the vegetables and sauce.

CHICKEN JARDINIÈRE

Jardinière *means "gardener" in French, and the vegetables change according to what is in season or in my garden. The stew is easy to put together, and it gets better every time you reheat it.*

2½ ounces lean pancetta, cut into lardons (strips about 1 inch long and ½ inch thick)

1½ tablespoons peanut oil

4 whole chicken legs (about 2¾ pounds), left whole or drumsticks and thighs separated, ends of the drumsticks and skin removed

1½ tablespoons all-purpose flour

1 teaspoon salt

1 teaspoon freshly ground black pepper

¾ cup fruity dry white wine

¾ cup water

12 small red potatoes (about 8 ounces), peeled

8 small baby bella or cremini mushrooms (about 5 ounces), washed

12 small pearl onions (about 4 ounces)

1¼ cups diced (1-inch) carrots

Sauté the lardons in the oil in a large saucepan or a Dutch oven (the pan should be wide enough to hold the chicken in a single layer) over high heat for 2 minutes. Add the chicken pieces and sauté them, turning once, for about 8 minutes, until lightly browned. Sprinkle with the flour, salt, and pepper and move the chicken around to distribute the flour evenly. Cook for 1 minute, then add the wine and water and mix well.

Add the potatoes, mushrooms, onions, carrots, garlic, and thyme and mix well. Bring to a full boil, making sure that the stew is boiling throughout, then cover, reduce the heat to low, and cook for 45 minutes. The stew can be prepared ahead to this point and reheated to serve.

At serving time, add the peas to the stew, bring to a boil, and boil for 2 minutes.

Transfer the stew to individual plates or a large platter, sprinkle with the parsley, and serve.

1½ tablespoons coarsely
    choppcd garlic

1 fresh thyme branch

1 cup frozen baby peas

2 tablespoons chopped fresh
    parsley

CHICKEN WITH SAFFRON RICE

SERVES 4

The dish is made with Arborio or other short-grain rice that I flavor with alcaparrado, *a mixture of olives, capers, and red pepper that is available in jars in specialty food stores and some supermarkets. You can make your own by mixing together equal portions of diced green olives, capers, and pimientos. Chicken legs stay moister than breasts and I remove the skin before cooking them, since it tends to become gummy.*

1 tablespoon olive oil

4 whole chicken legs (about 3 pounds), skin removed, drumsticks and thighs separated

3 cups thinly sliced onion

6 garlic cloves, coarsely chopped (2 tablespoons)

1½ cups Arborio or other short-grain rice

3 bay leaves

1 cup peeled, diced tomatoes

1½ cups alcaparrado (see above)

1½ tablespoons chopped jalapeño pepper (or more or less, depending on your tolerance for hotness)

1¼ teaspoons salt

1 teaspoon saffron threads

2½ cups water

Tabasco sauce (optional)

Heat the oil in a large skillet until hot. Add the chicken pieces in one layer and sauté over medium-high heat, turning occasionally, for 10 minutes, or until browned on all sides. Transfer the chicken to a plate and set aside.

Add the onions and garlic to the drippings in the skillet and cook for 2 minutes. Add the rice and mix well. Stir in the bay leaves, tomatoes, alcaparrado, jalapeño, salt, and saffron, add the water, and mix well.

Return the browned chicken pieces to the skillet, pushing them down into the liquid and rice until they are embedded in the mixture. Bring to a boil, reduce the heat to low, cover, and cook for 30 minutes, without stirring.

To serve, place a chicken thigh and drumstick, with some of the rice mixture, on each of four dinner plates. Sprinkle with Tabasco sauce, if desired, and serve.

SWEET-AND-SPICY CURRIED CHICKEN

SERVES 6

The spiciness of this curry is balanced by the sweetness of apple and banana, which lend smoothness and texture to the sauce. You can adjust the heat to your taste by increasing or decreasing the amount of cayenne and black pepper. Mint lends a refreshing quality. Although fresh mint is usually available at the supermarket, you can substitute dried if necessary. Serve with a pilaf. This dish is even better the next day.

1 tablespoon unsalted butter

1 tablespoon canola oil

6 whole chicken legs (about 3½ pounds), skin removed, drumsticks and thighs separated

2½ cups diced (½-inch) onion (12 ounces)

1 tablespoon all-purpose flour

2 tablespoons curry powder

1 teaspoon ground cumin

1½ teaspoons salt

1½ teaspoons freshly ground black pepper

¼ teaspoon cayenne pepper

5 garlic cloves, crushed and coarsely chopped (about 1½ tablespoons)

Heat the butter and oil in a large skillet until hot. Add the chicken pieces, in batches if necessary to prevent crowding, and sauté over medium-high heat, turning occasionally, until lightly browned on all sides, a total of about 7 minutes. Transfer the chicken to a large flameproof casserole.

Add the onion to the hot fat in the skillet and sauté over medium heat, stirring, for 2 to 3 minutes. Add the flour, curry powder, cumin, salt, black pepper, cayenne, and garlic and mix well. Add the water, stir, and bring to a boil. Pour the mixture over the chicken.

Add the apple, banana, and tomato to the chicken and bring to a boil over medium-high heat. Cover, reduce the heat, and simmer gently for 30 to 40 minutes. If using dried mint, crumble it over the chicken a few minutes before it is done.

If using fresh mint, sprinkle it on top of the chicken. Serve.

1 cup water

1 Granny Smith apple
  (8 ounces), unpeeled, halved,
  cored, and cut into 1-inch dice
  (about 1½ cups)

1 large firm but ripe banana,
  cut into ½-inch-thick slices

1 large tomato, cut into 1-inch
  cubes (about 1 cup)

2 tablespoons shredded fresh
  mint leaves or 1 teaspoon
  dried mint

GRILLED CHICKEN TENDERS WITH CHIMICHURRI

SERVES 4

Chimichurri sauce, originally from Argentina, is a finely chopped mixture of garlic, parsley, oil, and vinegar, usually served with beefsteak. In Mexico, it is made with cilantro and lime juice, and my version contains cilantro, scallions, radishes, and Mexican oregano. If chicken tenders are not available, cut up boneless, skinless chicken breasts for this recipe.

1¼ pounds chicken tenders
(about 16)

½ teaspoon salt

1 tablespoon olive oil

CHIMICHURRI SAUCE

½ cup coarsely chopped fresh
cilantro

⅓ cup minced scallions

1 tablespoon chopped garlic

½ cup julienned radishes

1 teaspoon dried oregano,
preferably Mexican

½ teaspoon hot pepper flakes

½ teaspoon salt

2 tablespoons fresh lime juice

⅓ cup olive oil

Preheat the oven to 140 degrees. Heat a grill to hot (or heat a nonstick skillet until very hot).

Put the tenders in a bowl, sprinkle with the salt and oil, and stir until well coated.

Arrange the chicken tenders on the hot grill (or in the hot skillet) and cook for about 1½ minutes. Turn and cook for 1 minute on the other side, or until just cooked through. Transfer to a platter and keep warm in the oven while you prepare the sauce.

Chimichurri Sauce: Mix all the ingredients together in a bowl.

Serve the chicken coated with the sauce.

GRILLED CHICKEN
WITH TARRAGON BUTTER

I prepare this dish inside on my stovetop gas grill in winter and outdoors on my gas or charcoal grill in summer. Make sure your grill is very clean, or the chicken will stick. The bird is grilled long enough so that most of the fat in the skin drains away, and it is then transferred to a warm oven to finish cooking in its own juices. A delicious tarragon butter, dotted on the chicken at serving time, replicates the flavor of a béarnaise sauce.

1 chicken (about 3 pounds), quartered, drumsticks and thighs separated

½ teaspoon salt

1 tablespoon olive oil

TARRAGON BUTTER

2 tablespoons unsalted butter, softened

1½ tablespoons olive oil

2 tablespoons chopped fresh tarragon

¼ teaspoon salt

2 teaspoons fresh lemon juice

Heat a grill until medium-hot. Preheat the oven to 160 degrees.

Sprinkle the chicken pieces with the salt and oil. Place the chicken skin side down on the clean hot grill. Grill the breasts for about 20 minutes and the leg pieces for about 30 minutes, turning occasionally, until nicely browned on all sides. As the chicken pieces are cooked, transfer them to a tray and put in the warm oven, uncovered, until ready to serve.

Tarragon Butter: Meanwhile, put all the ingredients in a blender or food processor and process until smooth.

Divide the chicken among four individual plates, dot each serving with about 1 tablespoon of the tarragon butter, and serve.

GRILLED CHICKEN WITH HERB SAUCE

An herb sauce adds flavor to the chicken and makes it look more luscious. It's always best to grill over hardwood charcoal or pieces of wood, not briquettes, but a gas grill will work almost as well.

1 chicken (3–3½ pounds), cut into 8 pieces (2 legs, 2 thighs, and 2 breasts, halved)

½ teaspoon salt

½ teaspoon freshly ground black pepper

1 tablespoon olive oil

SAUCE

2 tablespoons unsalted butter

2 garlic cloves, crushed and finely chopped (1 teaspoon)

⅓ cup chopped fresh herbs, such as thyme, rosemary, or savory

Pinch of salt

Pinch of freshly ground black pepper

⅓ cup Basic Brown Sauce (see opposite page)

Rub the chicken pieces with the salt, pepper, and olive oil and let marinate while you heat the grill.

Heat a grill until medium-hot.

Place the pieces of chicken skin side down on the hot grill and cook, turning the pieces every few minutes, for about 20 minutes for the wings and breasts, and up to 35 minutes for the legs and thighs. (If the heat is too high and the meat is cooking too fast, move the chicken to a cooler part of the grill or reduce the heat to low.)

Meanwhile, for the sauce: Melt the butter in a large skillet. Add the garlic and sauté for a few seconds. Add the herbs, salt, pepper, and brown sauce and bring to a boil, then reduce the heat to medium-low and cook for 1 minute.

As the pieces of chicken are cooked, coat each piece with the sauce and serve.

BASIC BROWN SAUCE

A basic and essential ingredient for the cook, brown sauce is added to other sauces or used to create a sauce for meat or poultry. Mine is slightly thickened with flour, which loses its raw taste through the long cooking process. The sauce can be made with all chicken bones or with turkey bones.

4 pounds veal or beef bones (shins, necks, tails, etc.), cut into 3-inch pieces (you can have the butcher do this)

1 pound chicken bones (necks, wings, backs, etc.)

2 cups diced onion

1 cup diced carrot

1 cup diced celery

6 garlic cloves, crushed but not peeled

⅓ cup all-purpose flour, dissolved in 1½ cups water

¼ cup tomato paste

8 quarts cold water

1 cup dry white wine

2 tablespoons dark soy sauce

1 teaspoon black peppercorns

3 bay leaves

1 teaspoon crushed dried thyme

Put the bones in a large stockpot and cook over high heat, stirring occasionally, for 15 minutes. Reduce over high heat, stirring occasionally, for 15 minutes. Reduce the heat to medium and cook for another 15 minutes, until they are browned and have rendered some fat. (There should be enough fat on the bones and in the skin to brown the bones.)

Add the onions, carrots, celery, and garlic and cook for another 15 minutes or so, stirring, until the bones and vegetables are lightly browned.

Drain the bones and vegetables in a colander to eliminate the fat and return them to the pot.

Add the flour mixture, tomato paste, water, wine, soy sauce, peppercorns, bay leaves, and thyme to the pot and bring to a boil, then reduce the heat and simmer slowly, uncovered, for about 3 hours, until reduced to about 8 cups. Skim off and discard the foam that comes to the top after 30 minutes. Strain the sauce through a fine strainer.

The sauce can be kept covered in the refrigerator for up to 1 week, or it can be divided among small plastic containers and frozen.

GRILLED CHICKEN WITH CABBAGE ANCHOÏADE

Chicken breasts are marinated in a finely chopped mixture of oregano, lemon rind, and black pepper and olive oil. Cooked on a hot grill, the breasts brown quickly but remain moist in the center. A mini-chop, smaller and faster than a food processor, is ideal for chopping the herbs and spices.

Anchoïade is a bold mixture of anchovy fillets, garlic, and olive oil that is combined here with cabbage and red bell pepper to serve as a bed for the chicken.

8 strips lemon rind, removed with a vegetable peeler, coarsely chopped

2 teaspoons black peppercorns

¼ cup loosely packed fresh oregano leaves

4 boneless, skinless chicken breasts (about 6 ounces each)

3 tablespoons olive oil

Combine the lemon rind, peppercorns, and oregano in a mini-chop and process to a coarse powder. (You should have about ¼ cup.)

Sprinkle the mixture over the chicken and arrange it in a dish. Drizzle with the oil. Cover and marinate in the refrigerator for at least 30 minutes. The chicken can marinate for as long as overnight.

CABBAGE ANCHOÏADE

½ red bell pepper, peeled and cut into ¼-inch dice (½ cup)

4 garlic cloves, crushed and finely chopped (about 2 teaspoons)

6 anchovy fillets, finely chopped

½ teaspoon salt

½ teaspoon freshly ground black pepper

4 teaspoons red wine vinegar

¼ cup olive oil

8 cups shredded savoy cabbage

1 teaspoon salt

Cabbage Anchoïade: Reserve 1 tablespoon of the red bell pepper for garnish. Combine the rest of the red pepper, the garlic, anchovies, salt, pepper, vinegar, and oil in a large bowl. Add the cabbage and mix well. The cabbage can be prepared up to 1 hour ahead and refrigerated until serving time.

Heat a grill until hot.

Sprinkle the chicken with the salt and arrange it on the clean hot grill. Cook for about 4 minutes on each side. Transfer to a plate.

Divide the cabbage mixture into a mound in the center of each of four serving plates. Slice the chicken breasts lengthwise into halves and arrange on top of the cabbage. Sprinkle with the reserved red pepper and serve.

ROAST STUFFED CORNISH HENS serves *4*

Nutty and wholesome, this bulgur wheat and leek stuffing works well with the hens' juices. Cornish hens are more elegant and easier to eat when boned first, but you can skip the boning if you like. The birds are cooked at such a high temperature that most of the fat in the skin collects in the bottom of the roasting pan. The fat is discarded and combined with the remaining drippings and a little water to form a sauce that is delicious with the hens.

Try to buy your bulgur in a health food store, where it is usually of better quality than that sold in the supermarket. Be sure to buy bulgur, not cracked wheat. The latter is uncooked; the former is cracked wheat that has been steamed and dried, and it needs only to be reconstituted in water.

⅓ cup bulgur wheat

2 Cornish hens (about 1¼ pounds each)

2 tablespoons canola oil

1 leek (4 ounces), trimmed (leaving some green), split, washed, and chopped (1¼ cups)

1 onion (4 ounces), chopped (about ¾ cup)

2 garlic cloves, crushed and chopped (about 1½ teaspoons)

1 teaspoon chopped jalapeño pepper (or more or less, depending on your tolerance for hotness)

Bring 1 cup water to a boil in a small saucepan. Stir in the bulgur and set the pan aside for 1 hour. Drain.

Preheat the oven to 425 degrees.

Bone the Cornish hens from the neck opening, without tearing the skin (see page 62; reserve the bones to make stock or soup). Set aside.

Heat 1 tablespoon of the oil in a large skillet. When it is hot, add the leek and onion and sauté for 2 to 3 minutes. Add the garlic and jalapeño and mix well. Stir in the apple, ⅜ teaspoon of the salt, the pepper, and bulgur. Mix well and cook, uncovered, over medium heat for 2 to 3 minutes, until any moisture in the wheat is absorbed and it is fluffy. Let cool.

Stuff the boned hens with the cooled apple and wheat mixture and tie the hens with kitchen twine to keep the stuffing inside.

1 Granny Smith apple, cored and cut into ⅜-inch pieces (about 1¼ cups)

½ teaspoon salt

½ teaspoon freshly ground black pepper

½ cup water

Place the hens in a roasting pan and spread the remaining 1 tablespoon oil on top. Sprinkle with the remaining ⅛ teaspoon salt. Roast for 40 minutes total, basting the hens with the juices and fat after 15 minutes and again after 30 minutes.

Remove the hens to a platter. Pour out and discard most of the fat that has accumulated in the roasting pan. Add the water to the pan and bring to a boil on the stovetop, stirring to melt the solidified juices in the bottom.

Cut the hens in half and remove the twine. Divide the juices among four plates, place half a hen on each plate, and serve.

🖤 How to Bone Cornish Hens and Other Small Birds

This technique for boning Cornish hens can also be used for squab or smaller birds such as partridge or woodcock.

Lift the skin at the neck of each Cornish hen and run your knife along either side of the wishbone. Then use your thumb and index finger to pry out the wishbone.

Cut through the shoulder joint on each side of the wishbone. Insert your index finger and thumb through the opening made by the knife and loosen the meat all around the carcass. The most delicate part of the operation is separating the skin from the back of the bird, as it adheres very tightly there and tends to tear: Carefully slide the tip of your index finger between the skin and the carcass to loosen the skin; go slowly to avoid tearing the skin.

After the meat has been separated from the back and shoulders, lift away the breast meat, using the knife to separate it from the top of the breastbone without tearing the skin. The fillets will still be attached to the carcass. When the meat is loosened from the breast-bone, turn the flesh inside out (like taking off socks), pulling the meat down and separating it from the carcass; keep pulling down until all the breast meat is separated and most of the carcass—up to the joint of the hip on each side—is visible.

Holding the Cornish hen by a thighbone, cut right through the hip joint and pull to separate the leg from the carcass. Repeat on the other side.

With the Cornish hen still inside out, scrape the meat from each thighbone with a knife, then cut all around the knee joint and keep scraping to release the meat from the drumstick bone. Break the bone at the foot; leave the knuckle in to hold the skin in place and prevent it from shrinking.

Cut off the wing bones on either side. Run your thumb along the carcass on each side of the breastbone and remove both fillets, pulling them off.

Turn the Cornish hen right side out. It is now completely boned, except for the knuckles.

Légumes

Artichoke Hearts with Tarragon
and Mushrooms · 66

Artichoke Hearts
and Peas · 68

Baby Artichokes with
Anchovies · 69

Asparagus Topped with Bread
Crumbs and Egg · 70

Asparagus in Mustard
Sauce · 72

Piquant Steamed Broccoli
with Lemon Sauce · 73

Fricassee of Brussels Sprouts
and Bacon · 74

Glazed Carrots with
Olives · 75

Carrots with Chives · 77

Cauliflower au Gratin · 78

Cauliflower Sauté à Cru · 79

Cauliflower à la
Polonaise · 80

Corn and Shallots with
Sun-Dried Tomatoes · 82

Crispy Corn Pancakes · 83

Cucumbers in Cream · 84

Eggplant Chinois · 85

Fried Eggplant Fans · 86

Eggplant and Tomato
Gratin · 88

Braised Endive · 89

Sautéed Haricots Verts
and Shallots · 90

Green Beans with Mustard
and Cream Dressing • 91

Leeks with Tomatoes
and Olive Oil • 92

Peas with Basil • 93

Peas à la Française • 94

Peas and Fennel
with Lardons • 95

Wild Mushroom Toasts • 96

Sautéed Potatoes with Parsley
and Garlic • 97

Small Potatoes in
Olive Oil • 98

Baker's Wife Potatoes • 99

Potatoes Rachael Ray • 100

Fluffy Mashed Potatoes • 101

Potato Gratin with
Cream • 102

Broiled Maple Sweet
Potatoes • 104

Pumpkin Gratin • 105

Velvet Spinach • 107

Classic Ratatouille • 108

Caramelized Tomatoes
Provençal • 110

Sliced Tomato Gratin • 111

Stuffed Tomatoes • 112

ARTICHOKE HEARTS WITH TARRAGON AND MUSHROOMS

SERVES *6* AS A
FIRST COURSE

I first prepared these artichokes at the home of my friend and mentor Helen McCully, a cookbook author and the food editor of House Beautiful, *in the early 1960s. Whipped cream is added to the sauce just before filling the hearts to add richness to the dish and give it a glaze when it is run under the broiler.*

2 tablespoons unsalted butter

2 cups mushrooms, cut into
½-inch dice (about 6 ounces)

1 tablespoon cognac

⅔ cup heavy cream

¼ teaspoon salt

⅛ teaspoon freshly ground
black pepper

1 tablespoon chopped mixed
fresh tarragon and parsley

½ teaspoon potato starch,
dissolved in 1 tablespoon
cold water

6 artichoke hearts, prepared
according to the directions in
the sidebar and kept warm
in the broth

1½ tablespoons freshly grated
Pecorino Romano cheese

Melt the butter in a large saucepan. Add the mushrooms and cook until the liquid from the mushrooms has evaporated. Add the cognac and cook for 30 seconds. Add ¼ cup of the cream, the salt, pepper, and herbs, and bring to a boil. Add the dissolved potato starch, mix well, and boil to thicken. Remove from the heat.

Preheat the broiler. Drain the artichoke hearts.

Whip the remaining cream until stiff. Rapidly fold into the mushroom mixture and immediately fill the artichoke hearts. Sprinkle with the cheese and place under the broiler for 2 to 3 minutes, until nicely browned. Serve.

🍠 How to Trim Artichoke Hearts

With a sharp knife, trim off all the outer leaves all around each artichoke heart, as close as you can without taking the "meat" out of the heart. Cut off the inner cone of leaves at the point where they attach to the choke. Cut off the stem. With a small knife or vegetable peeler, trim the remaining greenish leaves and smooth the bottom as well as you can. There should still be some light green flesh on the heart. Rub the heart with lemon and put in a stainless steel saucepan.

For 6 hearts, add 4 cups water, 2 table-spoons olive oil, 2 tablespoons fresh lemon juice, and ½ teaspoon salt. Bring to a boil, reduce the heat, and simmer for 30 to 40 min-utes until the hearts are tender when pierced with the point of a small knife. Remove from the heat.

When the hearts are cool enough to handle, remove the chokes with a spoon, then put the hearts in a container with enough of the cook-ing liquid to cover. They can be kept for at least 1 week in the refrigerator in the broth.

ARTICHOKE HEARTS AND PEAS

I love frozen baby peas, which are the smallest, sweetest peas. Frozen artichokes are another favorite. I always keep both on hand, so I can put this dish together whenever I have to feed unexpected guests.

3 tablespoons olive oil

¼ cup chopped onion

1 tablespoon chopped garlic

2 teaspoons all-purpose flour

¾ cup homemade chicken stock, low-sodium canned chicken broth, or water

2 teaspoons chopped fresh savory or thyme

1 9-ounce package frozen artichoke hearts

1 10-ounce package frozen baby peas

¾ teaspoon salt

½ teaspoon freshly ground black pepper

Heat the oil in a large saucepan. Add the onion and garlic and sauté for 1 minute. Sprinkle on the flour, mix well, and cook for 30 seconds. Add the stock or water and savory or thyme and bring to a boil, stirring occasionally.

Add the artichokes and peas (frozen or defrosted), salt, and pepper, mix well, and bring to a boil (this will take longer if the vegetables were frozen when added). Cover, reduce the heat to low, and cook for 2 to 3 minutes. Serve.

BABY ARTICHOKES WITH ANCHOVIES

This is one of my favorite ways of serving small or baby artichokes. They are cooked with wine and garlic, then anchovies are added and they are served lukewarm as a first course or side dish. The smaller the artichokes, the better, because the chokes will not have started forming in the center.

2 pounds baby artichokes (about 20)

2 tablespoons olive oil

¾ teaspoon salt

½ teaspoon freshly ground black pepper

½ teaspoon fennel seeds

3 strips lemon rind, removed with a vegetable peeler

1½ cups coarsely chopped onion (6 ounces)

5 garlic cloves, thinly sliced (1 tablespoon)

½ cup dry white wine

½ cup water

1 2-ounce can anchovies in oil, coarsely chopped

1 tablespoon chopped fresh chives

Cut off the top half of each artichoke and discard. Cut around each artichoke about ¼ inch deep to remove the tough outside leaves. Cut the artichokes in half.

Combine all the ingredients except the anchovies and chives in a large stainless steel saucepan, bring to a boil, and boil, covered, for about 15 minutes, or until the artichokes are tender and most of the cooking liquid has evaporated.

Mix in the anchovies and bring back to a boil, then remove from the heat.

Serve the artichokes lukewarm, garnished with the chives.

ASPARAGUS TOPPED WITH BREAD CRUMBS AND EGG

SERVES 4

I always buy large asparagus with tight heads and firm stalks. I peel the lower third of each stalk so the entire spear is tender. My wife and I love asparagus steamed and served cold with a mustard vinaigrette or warm with hollandaise sauce or melted butter, as well as in gratins with a white sauce and cheese crust. In this recipe, I serve it just warm, topped with crunchy bread crumbs, chopped egg, and scallions. The fried bread crumbs are also great on top of salads, soups, or pasta.

1¼ pounds large asparagus spears with tight heads (16–20)

¾ teaspoon salt

2 slices white bread, cut into ¼-inch pieces (about 1¼ cups)

2 tablespoons unsalted butter

1 tablespoon canola oil

3 tablespoons minced scallions

Peel the lower third of each asparagus spear and cut the spears into 2-inch pieces. (You should have about 4 cups.)

Pour 1 cup water into a large skillet, add ¼ teaspoon of the salt, and bring the water to a boil. Add the asparagus, cover, and bring back to a boil (this should take about 2 minutes). Cook for another 2 minutes. Transfer to a plate to drain and let the asparagus cool.

Process the bread to crumbs in a food processor. (You should have about 1 cup.)

Melt the butter with the canola oil in a small skillet. Add the bread crumbs and stir with a spoon so the bread is moistened with the butter and oil; the mixture will be soft. Keep

½ teaspoon freshly ground
black pepper

1 tablespoon olive oil

1 large hard-cooked egg,
chopped with an egg slicer or
a sharp knife

Minced fresh chives (optional)

cooking and stirring the bread for about 2 minutes. Add the
scallions and cook, stirring and sautéing, until the mixture
gets drier. Then cook for about 2 minutes longer, still stirring,
until the crumbs are nicely browned and dry. Transfer the
crumbs to a plate.

At serving time, sprinkle the asparagus with the remaining ½ teaspoon salt, the pepper, and the olive oil. Heat for
about 1½ minutes in a microwave oven, or until the asparagus is warm.

Divide the asparagus among four plates, sprinkle on the
bread crumbs, chopped egg, and chives, if using, and serve
immediately.

ASPARAGUS IN MUSTARD SAUCE

SERVES 4 AS A FIRST COURSE

This is the classic asparagus and mustard vinaigrette of French bistros and family restaurants. As a child, I would place a spoon or fork under my plate when eating it so the pungent vinaigrette collected at the lower edge of the plate. That way, I could dip the tips of the spears and my bread into the sauce before eating them. Not an elegant table maneuver, but effective.

I peel the asparagus stalks for this recipe and boil them in just enough water so that most of it evaporates by the time the asparagus is cooked. Serve at room temperature.

1¼ pounds large asparagus spears (16–20), trimmed and peeled (see sidebar)

SAUCE

2 tablespoons Dijon mustard

2 tablespoons canola oil

2 tablespoons walnut oil

2 teaspoons white wine vinegar

½ teaspoon salt

¼ teaspoon freshly ground black pepper

Put the asparagus in a large stainless steel saucepan in one or two layers and add ¾ cup boiling water. Cover, bring to a boil, and boil for 3 minutes, or until the asparagus is just tender but still firm and most of the liquid has evaporated. Drain off any remaining water and put the asparagus on a platter. Let cool.

Sauce: Combine all the ingredients in a small bowl and mix well; do not worry if the mixture is not totally emulsified.

Serve the asparagus with the sauce.

♥ **How to Trim Asparagus**

So that the whole spear will be tender, peel the lower half of the stalk using a vegetable peeler: Holding the asparagus by the bottom end, peel it from the base of the tip down to your fingers, rotating the stem as you peel. Cut or break off the unpeeled bottom part of the stalk.

PIQUANT STEAMED BROCCOLI WITH LEMON SAUCE

SERVES 4

Steamed briefly so that it keeps its texture and deep green color, the broccoli is tossed with a simple sauce made of lemon juice, olive oil, and Tabasco. This dish can be served as a first course or a side.

SAUCE

1½ tablespoons fresh lemon juice

¼ cup extra-virgin olive oil

¼ teaspoon Tabasco sauce

¼ teaspoon salt

1½ pounds broccoli

Sauce: Combine the lemon juice, olive oil, Tabasco, and salt in a bowl. Mix well and set aside.

Cut the broccoli florets from the stems and separate into 2-inch-wide florets. Peel the stems and cut them into strips about ½ inch thick by 2 inches long.

Arrange the broccoli florets and stems on a heatproof plate, place in a steamer, and steam, covered, over boiling water for 11 to 12 minutes, until tender.

Toss gently with the sauce and serve.

FRICASSEE OF BRUSSELS SPROUTS AND BACON

For many years, I cooked Brussels sprouts in salted water and then sautéed them whole or halved in butter, seasoning them with a little salt and pepper. They were good, but not extraordinary. This recipe, however, gives fantastic results. I slice the sprouts raw in my food processor and sauté them with bacon bits. The whole process takes fewer than 10 minutes. When buying your sprouts, remember to buy enough so the trimmed weight is about 1 pound: 1¼ pounds should do it.

1 pound trimmed and cleaned Brussels sprouts

4 slices bacon, cut crosswise into ¼-inch pieces (about ¾ cup)

2 tablespoons good olive oil

½ teaspoon salt

½ teaspoon freshly ground black pepper

Using the slicing blade on your food processor, cut the Brussels sprouts into slices about ¼ inch thick. (You should have about 5 cups.)

Scatter the bacon pieces in a large skillet, add the oil, cover, and cook over high heat for 2 to 3 minutes, until the pieces are crisp and brown and most of the fat is rendered. Add the sliced sprouts, salt, and pepper, cover, and cook for 1 to 2 minutes to soften the sprouts. Uncover and cook over high heat, tossing occasionally, for about 2 minutes, until the sprouts are tender but still a bit firm. Serve.

GLAZED CARROTS WITH OLIVES

Combined with salt, a bit of sugar, butter, and water, baby carrots are cooked until the moisture evaporates and they begin to glaze. They are finished with olives and capers.

1 pound baby carrots, peeled

1 teaspoon sugar

¼ teaspoon salt

1 tablespoon unsalted butter

½ cup oil-cured black olives, pitted

2 tablespoons drained capers

2 teaspoons minced fresh chives

Combine the carrots, sugar, salt, butter, and ⅔ cup water in a heavy saucepan, cover, and cook over high heat for about 8 minutes, until all the water is gone and the carrots are tender and starting to glaze. (If some moisture remains in the pan when the carrots are tender, cook them, uncovered, for 2 to 3 minutes to evaporate the water so they glaze lightly on all sides.)

Add the olives and capers and cook for 1 minute, just long enough to heat the olives through. Sprinkle with the chives and serve.

CARROTS WITH CHIVES

Thinly sliced carrots cook in just a few minutes. They can be sliced ahead but are best sautéed at the last moment. By the time the liquid evaporates, the carrots will have glazed in the butter, oil, and sugar.

5–6 large carrots (about 1 pound), peeled

1 tablespoon unsalted butter

1 tablespoon peanut or canola oil

½ teaspoon salt

½ teaspoon sugar

¼ cup water

¼ cup chopped shallots

½ teaspoon freshly ground black pepper

2 tablespoons minced fresh chives

Using a mandoline or a knife, slice the carrots into ⅔-inch slices. (You should have about 3½ cups.) Combine the carrots, butter, and oil in a skillet. Sprinkle the carrots with the salt and sugar, add the water, and cook, covered, for about 3 minutes over high heat. Add the shallots and pepper and cook, covered, for about 2 minutes.

Add the chives and cook for about 1 minute, uncovered, until the pan is dry, tossing the carrots occasionally. Serve.

CAULIFLOWER AU GRATIN

Made with a béchamel sauce and finished with cheese, this cauliflower dish is one I remember well from my childhood.

1 cauliflower (about 1½ pounds)

3 tablespoons unsalted butter

3 tablespoons all-purpose flour

1½ cups milk

¾ cup heavy cream

½ teaspoon salt

¼ teaspoon freshly ground white pepper

⅛ teaspoon freshly grated nutmeg

½ cup grated Gruyère or Emmenthaler cheese

2 tablespoons freshly grated Parmesan cheese

Preheat the oven to 400 degrees.

Trim the green leaves and cut out the core from the cauliflower; separate it into florets. Drop the florets into a large stainless steel saucepan of boiling salted water, bring back to a boil, and cook, uncovered, for about 5 minutes; they will be crunchy. Drain and set aside.

Melt the butter in a medium saucepan. Add the flour and cook over low heat for about 1 minute, stirring with a whisk; do not let the mixture brown. Add the milk and bring to a boil over medium heat, stirring constantly to prevent scorching, then simmer over low heat for 1 minute. Add the cream, salt, white pepper, and nutmeg and bring to a boil. Remove from the heat.

Generously butter a gratin dish. Put the florets in the dish stem side down and coat with the béchamel. Sprinkle with the cheeses. Place on a baking sheet and bake for about 30 minutes, or until golden brown. Serve.

CAULIFLOWER SAUTÉ À CRU

SERVES 4

Here, the whole cauliflower head is quartered, then sliced and sautéed in olive oil. No precooking is required, and the cauliflower has a clean, fresh taste. There will be some cauliflower "crumbs" when you slice it; they should be sautéed along with the slices. Hazelnut oil gives the dish a wonderful nutty taste. If it is unavailable, use peanut oil.

1 cauliflower (1½ to 2 pounds)

3 tablespoons extra-virgin olive oil

1 tablespoon hazelnut oil

½ teaspoon salt

½ teaspoon freshly ground black pepper

2 teaspoons chopped garlic (about 3 cloves)

¼ cup minced fresh chives

Trim the green leaves and core, and cut the cauliflower through the stem into quarters. Cut each quarter into ½-inch slices. You will have about 16 slices, plus crumbs.

Divide the oils between two large (12-inch) skillets, preferably nonstick, and heat the oil. (If you have only one large skillet, cook the cauliflower in two batches, using half the oil for each batch.) Add the cauliflower slices in one layer (with the crumbs) and cook over high heat for about 5 minutes, until browned on the bottom. Turn the cauliflower and cook for another 4 minutes, or until lightly browned on the second side.

Add the salt, pepper, garlic, and chives, stir to combine, and cook for another minute. Serve.

CAULIFLOWER À LA POLONAISE

SERVES 6

Sautéed cauliflower florets can simply be tossed with butter, toasted bread crumbs, and chopped egg, but reassembling the florets into a head of cauliflower and garnishing it is nice for an elegant dinner party. The classic egg and bread crumb garnish is called polonaise.

1 large or 2 small firm white cauliflower (about 3½ pounds total)

8 tablespoons (1 stick) unsalted butter

1 tablespoon olive oil

1 teaspoon salt

¼ teaspoon freshly ground white pepper

1 large hard-cooked egg, finely chopped

2 tablespoons chopped fresh parsley

1 large slice firm white bread, processed to crumbs in a food processor (¾ cup)

Bring a large pot of salted water to a boil. Meanwhile, cut the green leaves from the cauliflower and separate the florets by cutting around the core(s) with a knife.

Place the florets in the boiling water and bring the water to a boil again; reduce the heat and boil gently for 6 to 8 minutes, until the stems are tender when pierced with the point of a knife. Drain.

Melt half of the butter in a very large heavy skillet. (If you don't have an extra-large skillet, use two.) Add the oil. When the mixture is hot, carefully place the florets head down in it, sprinkle with the salt and white pepper, and cook over medium-low heat for 5 to 7 minutes, until the florets are golden brown.

If you'd like to present the florets as a reassembled head of cauliflower (or 2 heads), arrange in the following way: Make a circle of florets—5 to 6 inches in diameter—on a dinner plate (or on each of two plates), with the stems pointing toward the center. Continue building up by placing florets, stems always pointed down, in smaller and smaller circles until the construction resembles a head of cauliflower. Mix the chopped egg and parsley together and sprinkle on the cauliflower.

Melt the remaining butter in a skillet. Add the bread crumbs and cook, shaking the skillet constantly, until the crumbs are golden brown. Pour over the cauliflower and serve.

Alternatively, toss the sautéed florets with the chopped egg and parsley, sprinkle with the toasted bread crumbs, and serve.

CORN AND SHALLOTS
WITH SUN-DRIED TOMATOES

SERVES 4

Like most people, my wife and I usually eat local fresh sweet corn on the cob, just steamed for a few seconds over boiling water. But when the urge for a change hits during corn season, I remove the kernels for use in fritters and soup, or simply sauté them, as here.

4 ears sweet corn, as young and fresh as possible, husked

1 tablespoon peanut oil

1 tablespoon unsalted butter

¼ cup chopped shallots

¼ teaspoon salt

½ teaspoon freshly ground black pepper

¼ cup diced (½-inch) sun-dried tomatoes in oil

¼ teaspoon coarsely chopped fresh cilantro

Using a sharp knife or a mandoline, slice the kernels off the ears of corn. (You should have about 3 cups kernels.) Heat the oil and butter in a large skillet until very hot. Add the shallots and sauté for 30 seconds, then add the corn kernels and cook over high heat, tossing, for about 2½ minutes. Add the salt, pepper, tomatoes, and cilantro and cook for about 30 seconds longer.

Mix well and serve.

CRISPY CORN PANCAKES

SERVES 6 (MAKES ABOUT SIXTEEN 3-INCH PANCAKES)

Serve these pancakes as an hors d'oeuvre or a first course or as an accompaniment to pork.

It's important to use a nonstick pan and very hot oil for cooking them; canola oil can withstand high temperatures without burning. For best results, the pan should be cleaned between each batch of pancakes.

When you prepare the batter, you add only half of the club soda at first to the flour and egg mixture, to create a thick batter that you make very smooth with a whisk before adding the remainder of the club soda. If you put it in all at once, the flour will form into little lumps and the batter will have to be strained.

Although the pancakes are best when made at the last moment, they can be made ahead and reheated in a hot oven or under the broiler.

⅔ cup all-purpose flour

¾ teaspoon baking powder

1 large egg

2 large ears corn, husked and kernels cut off (about 2 cups)

1 cup chilled club soda

¼ teaspoon salt

¼ teaspoon freshly ground black pepper

½ cup canola oil

Combine the flour, baking powder, egg, corn kernels, and half of the club soda in a food processor and process for 10 seconds. Add the remaining club soda, the salt, and pepper and process for a few seconds, until well combined. Transfer to a bowl.

At cooking time, heat 2 tablespoons of the oil in a large nonstick skillet. When it is hot, spoon 3 tablespoons of batter per pancake into the skillet, making 4 pancakes. (To make the pancakes faster, use two skillets.) Use a splatter-guard if you have one and cook the pancakes over high heat for 3 minutes, then turn them and cook for 2 minutes on the other side, or until crispy at the edges and brown. Transfer the pancakes to a wire rack (the rack allows air to circulate under them, so they won't become soggy). Wipe out the skillet and repeat with the remaining oil and batter in batches. Serve.

CUCUMBERS IN CREAM

These are great with poached fish, such as salmon.

- 4 cucumbers (about 3½ pounds)
- 1 tablespoon unsalted butter
- ½ teaspoon salt
- ¼ teaspoon freshly ground white pepper
- ⅓ cup heavy cream
- 2 tablespoons chopped fresh chives

Peel the cucumbers and cut lengthwise into quarters. Remove and discard the seeds. Then cut the quarters into 1½- to 2-inch chunks.

Melt the butter in a large skillet. Add the cucumbers, salt, and white pepper and sauté over medium heat for 1 minute. Add the cream and boil over medium-high heat until it is reduced and thick enough to coat the cucumbers, 3 to 4 minutes. Sprinkle with the chives and serve.

EGGPLANT CHINOIS

The beauty of many Chinese dishes is the use of bottled sauces, which I always have on hand in my refrigerator or pantry. The eggplants are cut into chunks, sautéed in oil, and finished with garlic, ginger, and several of these sauces. This is a nice dish to serve with a roast.

1 tablespoon dark soy sauce

1 tablespoon oyster sauce

1 tablespoon hoisin sauce

2 teaspoons hot chili sauce, such as Sriracha

⅓ cup water

4 small, narrow (about 1½ inches in diameter) Japanese or Chinese eggplants (about 1 pound)

2 tablespoons canola oil

1 tablespoon chopped garlic

1 tablespoon chopped peeled ginger

⅓ cup sliced (½-inch) scallions

¼ cup coarsely chopped fresh cilantro

Mix the soy sauce, oyster sauce, hoisin sauce, hot chili sauce, and water together in a small bowl. Set aside. Slice the eggplant crosswise 1¼ inches thick, then slice the disks into wedges. (You should have about 4 cups.)

Heat the oil in a large skillet. Add the eggplant and sauté over high heat, covered, for about 7 minutes, turning the pieces in the hot oil occasionally. Remove the lid, add the garlic, ginger, and scallions, and sauté, uncovered, for about 1 minute, tossing the mixture a few times.

Add the soy sauce mixture to the skillet, cover, and cook for about 1 minute. Uncover and cook for 1 minute longer, then add the cilantro, toss, and serve.

FRIED EGGPLANT FANS

For this recipe, I use the long, thin, deep red or bright purple eggplant variously called Japanese, Chinese, or Asian eggplant. They are firm with small seeds. Each eggplant is split lengthwise in half, and then the halves are cut into thin slices still attached at one end; when spread out and fried, they look like beautiful, crisp brown fans. The fans are good as a garnish for grilled meat or poultry, as an appetizer, or on a salad. They are best eaten right out of the skillet, but you can keep them for 10 or 15 minutes if you arrange them in one layer on a wire rack, so they don't get soggy underneath, and put them in a warm oven.

The batter should be very cold to produce the crispiest coating.

2 Japanese or Chinese eggplants (about 6 ounces each, 8 to 10 inches long and 2 inches thick), tops trimmed

BATTER

2 large egg yolks

½ cup all-purpose flour

¾ cup ice-cold water

About ½ cup canola oil, for frying

Salt

Cut each eggplant lengthwise in half on a diagonal on a cutting board, so one end of each half eggplant is thicker than the other end. To make the fans, turn a half eggplant cut side down with the thick end toward you and cut lengthwise into thin slices (about ¼ inch thick), cutting from the thin end to the thick end and leaving the slices attached at the thin end. You should get 7 or 8 slices. Press on the slices to spread them out to create a fan about 6 inches wide at the wide end. Repeat with the remaining eggplant halves.

Batter: Mix the egg yolks, flour, and ¼ cup of the ice water with a whisk in a bowl to make a thick, smooth batter. Add the remaining ½ cup ice water and mix it in. (If making the batter ahead, refrigerate.)

At cooking time, heat the oil in two large nonstick skillets (or fry in two batches, using half the oil for each one). Dip each fan into the batter so it is well coated on both sides, place 2 of them, in one layer, in the hot oil in each skillet, and press lightly to make the fans spread out. Cook over high heat for about 4 minutes on the first side, then turn over and cook for 3 to 4 minutes on the other side, until cooked through, crisp, and well browned on both sides.

Using a spatula, transfer the eggplant to a wire rack. Sprinkle with salt and serve. Or keep warm on the rack in a 145 degree oven for a few minutes, until ready to serve.

EGGPLANT AND TOMATO GRATIN *SERVES 4*

Lightly oiling slices of eggplant, spreading them out on a baking sheet, and baking them is easier than cooking them in batches in a skillet and requires much less oil. The slices are then layered with tomatoes in a gratin dish, topped with flavored bread crumbs, and finished in the oven.

2 long, narrow Japanese or Chinese eggplants (1 pound)

2 tablespoons corn oil

½ teaspoon salt

1 large slice firm white bread, processed to crumbs in a food processor (⅔ cup)

⅓ cup freshly grated Parmesan cheese

1 teaspoon chopped fresh thyme

1 tablespoon olive oil

4 medium ripe tomatoes (about 1 pound), cut into ⅜-inch-thick slices

Preheat the oven to 400 degrees.

Trim the ends of the eggplants (do not peel) and cut them lengthwise into ½-inch-thick slices. (You should have 8 slices.)

Line a baking sheet with a nonstick baking mat and coat the mat with the corn oil. Lay the eggplant slices in a single layer in the oil and turn them over in the pan so they are lightly oiled on both sides. Sprinkle the slices with the salt. Bake for 25 minutes. Let the eggplant cool to lukewarm. (Leave the oven on.)

Meanwhile, mix the bread crumbs, Parmesan cheese, thyme, and olive oil in a small bowl.

Arrange alternating slices of eggplant and tomato in a 4- to 6-cup gratin dish, overlapping the slices as necessary to fit them all into the dish. Sprinkle the bread crumb mixture evenly on top. (At this point, the dish can be covered and refrigerated overnight.)

Bake the gratin for 20 to 25 minutes, until the vegetables are soft and heated through and the crumb topping is nicely browned. Serve.

BRAISED ENDIVE

Braised endive is a delicious accompaniment to stews or roast meats. Wrapping it in slices of ham, covering it with a light cream sauce and cheese, and glazing it under the broiler transforms it into endive Flemish-style.

2 pounds Belgian endives (8 medium), trimmed of any damaged leaves

Rind of 1 lemon, removed with a vegetable peeler

1 tablespoon fresh lemon juice

4 tablespoons (½ stick) unsalted butter

2 teaspoons sugar

1 teaspoon salt

¾ cup water

Arrange the endives in a large stainless steel or enameled cast-iron pot that holds them tightly. Add the lemon rind, lemon juice, 2 tablespoons of the butter, the sugar, salt, and water. Cover with a round of parchment paper cut to fit, so that the steam that rises during cooking will just touch the paper and fall back on the endives (this makes for a moister dish and prevents the endives from discoloring). Place a plate that fits inside the pot upside down on top to keep the endives submerged in their juices, cover with a lid, and bring to a boil. Reduce the heat to low and boil gently for 15 to 20 minutes, until the endives are tender. (The endives can be cooked ahead and set aside in a warm spot.)

Remove the endives from the liquid, drain, and arrange on a platter. Melt the remaining 2 tablespoons butter, pour over the endives, and serve.

SAUTÉED HARICOTS VERTS AND SHALLOTS

SERVES 4

This harmonious combination of green beans, shallots, and butter is a winner. Try to get authentic haricots verts, *thin very young green beans—available in specialty food stores or at farmers' markets—or choose the smallest, firmest regular string beans you can find. Make sure to cook them fully; they should be tender, not crunchy. Too often beans are just blanched, and their taste is not what it should be.*

1 pound haricots verts or very small string beans, tips removed

1 tablespoon unsalted butter

1 tablespoon peanut oil

2 tablespoons finely chopped shallots

¼ teaspoon salt

¼ teaspoon freshly ground black pepper

Bring 1½ cups water to a boil in a large saucepan. Add the beans and cook, covered, over high heat for 7 to 8 minutes, until they are tender but still firm to the bite. Drain the beans and spread them on a large platter to cool.

At serving time, heat the butter and oil in a large skillet. When they are hot, add the shallots and sauté for about 10 seconds. Add the beans, salt, and pepper and sauté for about 2 minutes, until the beans are heated through. Serve.

GREEN BEANS WITH MUSTARD AND CREAM DRESSING

SERVES 4

Most cooks undercook string beans nowadays, but the true taste comes out only if they are cooked through. Small, thin haricots verts are very good here, but larger string beans are also fine if they are deep green in color and firm and snap when broken. The cream and mustard dressing is a standard at our house. If it is made an hour or so before serving, it will thicken considerably; add 1 to 2 tablespoons of water to the dressing at serving time to thin it to a creamy consistency.

½ teaspoon salt

1 pound haricots verts or green beans

DRESSING

2 tablespoons Dijon mustard

¼ cup heavy cream

½ teaspoon salt

½ teaspoon freshly ground black pepper

2 tablespoons finely chopped shallots

1 large tomato (about 8 ounces), cut into 8 slices, each slice halved

2 tablespoons coarsely chopped fresh parsley

Pour 6 cups water into a large saucepan, add the salt, and bring to a boil. Meanwhile, trim the ends from the beans. Add the beans to the boiling salted water and bring back to a boil. (This will take about 2 minutes.) Cook the beans for 4 to 5 minutes, until they are tender but still firm. Drain.

Dressing: Combine all the ingredients in a bowl large enough to hold the beans. Add the lukewarm beans to the dressing, thinning it first with 1 or 2 tablespoons water if needed, and mix well.

Divide the beans among four plates and surround each serving with 4 half slices of tomato to make a border. Sprinkle with the parsley and serve.

LEEKS WITH TOMATOES AND OLIVE OIL

SERVES 4 AS A FIRST COURSE

Cooked until just tender, these leeks are served with a tangy sauce flavored with diced tomatoes, olive oil, and Dijon mustard. Serve them at room temperature.

Keep the water that you boil the leeks in for use in soups; it has a wonderfully intense flavor.

4 medium to large leeks (about 1¼ pounds), trimmed (leaving most of the green), split, and washed

1 ripe tomato (about 7 ounces), peeled, halved, seeded, and cut into ¼-inch pieces

3 tablespoons olive oil

1 tablespoon red wine vinegar

1 tablespoon Dijon mustard

1 teaspoon Worcestershire sauce

½ teaspoon salt

¼ teaspoon freshly ground black pepper

Bring 2 cups water to a boil in a large saucepan. Add the leeks and bring back to a boil, then reduce the heat and boil gently, covered, for 15 minutes, or until tender. Drain (reserve the liquid for soup, if you like).

When they are cool enough to handle, squeeze the leeks to extract most of the remaining liquid (reserve it with the rest of the liquid). Cut the leeks into 2-inch pieces and arrange them in a gratin dish, mixing the white and green parts.

Mix together the tomato, oil, vinegar, mustard, Worcestershire, salt, and pepper. Spoon over the leeks. Serve at room temperature.

PEAS WITH BASIL

There is nothing better than fresh peas just out of the pod in late spring, and they are always worth a special trip to a local farm or farmers' market when they're in season. (Frozen baby peas make a fine substitute at other times of year.) Basil is plentiful in my summer garden, and this dish is a delicious variation on the old favorite of peas and mint.

1 pound (3 cups) shelled small fresh peas (about 6 pounds peas in the pod) or frozen baby peas, thawed

2½ tablespoons unsalted butter

¾ teaspoon sugar

¾ teaspoon salt

½ teaspoon freshly ground black pepper

⅓ cup water

⅓ cup shredded fresh basil

Combine the peas, butter, sugar, salt, pepper, and water in a saucepan, bring to a boil, and boil over high heat for about 5 minutes, stirring occasionally, until most of the water has evaporated and the peas are tender. Add the basil, mix well, and serve.

PEAS À LA FRANÇAISE

In this classic dish, Boston lettuce and tiny pearl onions are cooked with a dash of oil and water, then peas are added and cooked for a little longer. If fresh peas are not available, frozen baby peas work well. Boston lettuce is the best for this recipe. It remains slightly crunchy, with a hint of bitterness that goes well with the onions and peas. Potato starch can be found in the baking section of most supermarkets.

8 ounces small pearl onions (about 24), peeled

½ teaspoon herbes de Provence

1 tablespoon sugar

1 teaspoon salt

¼ teaspoon freshly ground black pepper

2 tablespoons olive oil

1 cup water

1 small head Boston lettuce (8 ounces), washed and cut into 2-inch pieces

1½ pounds fresh peas, shelled (about 2½ cups), or 2½ cups frozen baby peas

1 teaspoon potato starch dissolved in 1 tablespoon water

1 tablespoon unsalted butter

Combine the onions, herbes de Provence, sugar, salt, pepper, oil, and water in a saucepan and bring to a boil, then reduce the heat, cover, and cook for 5 minutes. Add the lettuce, and cook, covered, for 3 to 4 minutes longer, until the lettuce has wilted. (The dish can be made ahead to this point. Reheat before proceeding.)

Add the peas to the lettuce mixture and bring to a boil. Boil for about 5 minutes if using fresh peas (adjusting the timing as required based on the size of the peas) or 2 minutes if using frozen peas.

Mix in the dissolved potato starch and bring back to a boil to thicken the juices. Mix in the butter and serve.

PEAS AND FENNEL WITH LARDONS

SERVES 4

The combination of fennel, with its slightly licorice flavor, and salt pork complements the sweetness of the peas. This is an ideal accompaniment to grilled meats.

4 ounces lean cured pork or pancetta, cut into ¾-inch pieces

2 cups water

2 cups coarsely chopped onion

2 cups diced (1-inch) fennel (about 8 ounces)

1 tablespoon coarsely chopped garlic

8 ounces (1½ cups) shelled small fresh peas (about 3 pounds peas in the pod) or frozen baby peas

½ teaspoon salt

¼ teaspoon sugar

½ teaspoon freshly ground black pepper

1 tablespoon olive oil

1 tablespoon unsalted butter

Put the pork or pancetta in a large saucepan. Add the water and bring to a boil over high heat. Cover, reduce the heat to low, and boil gently for 10 minutes. There should be about 1¼ cups of liquid left in the pan.

Add the onion, fennel, and garlic and bring to a boil. Reduce the heat and boil gently for about 8 minutes.

Add the peas, salt, sugar, pepper, oil, and butter and bring to a boil. Boil, uncovered, for about 3 minutes to cook the peas and reduce the liquid. Serve.

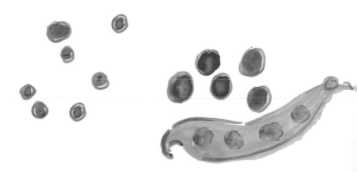

WILD MUSHROOM TOASTS

I often go mushrooming in the woods with my wife and daughter, my friends, or sometimes just my dog. For this dish, one of my favorite summer first courses, I use a mixture of domestic and wild mushrooms and spoon them over toast. The mushrooms are also good on the side with steak or grilled veal or lamb chops.

If you don't know wild mushrooms, do not pick them on your own, since some are toxic. Mycological societies throughout the country organize tours, however. If this activity appeals to you, contact the society nearest to you, and go on a hunt with people who are knowledgeable. It's great fun, and the wild mushrooms you find yourself are free!

2 tablespoons unsalted butter

1 tablespoon olive oil

1 pound mixed cultivated and wild mushrooms (such as cèpes/porcini, chanterelles, and oyster mushrooms), cleaned and cut into 2-inch pieces or left whole, depending on size

4 shallots, thinly sliced (½ cup)

½ cup chopped mixed fresh oregano, chives, and parsley

½ teaspoon salt

½ teaspoon freshly ground black pepper

4 slices firm country bread, each about 4 inches in diameter and ½ inch thick

Extra-virgin olive oil, for garnish (optional)

Heat the butter and olive oil in a large skillet until very hot and hazelnut in color. Add the mushrooms and sauté over high heat for 10 seconds. Cover and continue cooking for 3 minutes. Uncover and cook for 2 to 3 minutes, until the liquid the mushrooms released has evaporated. Add the shallots, herbs, salt, and pepper and cook for 1 minute longer.

Meanwhile, toast the slices of bread and arrange them on a plate.

Spoon the mushroom mixture on top of the toasts, sprinkle a little extra-virgin olive oil on top, if desired, and serve.

SAUTÉED POTATOES
WITH PARSLEY AND GARLIC

SERVES 4

*These are standard on bistro menus. Don't cook them ahead, or they will soften and lose
the crisp exterior that contrasts so well with their soft insides. They can, however, be
peeled and cut into cubes in advance and covered with water so they don't discolor. Just
before cooking, drain and dry them with paper towels.*

3 large Red Bliss potatoes
  (18 ounces), peeled

3 tablespoons canola oil

3 garlic cloves

¼ cup loosely packed fresh
  parsley leaves

½ teaspoon salt

½ teaspoon freshly ground
  black pepper

Cut the potatoes into ⅜-inch cubes. Put in a sieve and rinse
well under cool water. Transfer to a bowl, add water to cover,
and set aside until ready to cook.

Heat the oil in a large nonstick skillet. Drain the potatoes, pat dry with paper towels, and add to the hot oil. Sauté
over high heat for 12 to 14 minutes, stirring occasionally,
until the potatoes are browned on all sides.

Meanwhile, chop the garlic and parsley together until
finely minced.

Add the salt, pepper, and parsley mixture to the potatoes
in the skillet, tossing to combine. Serve.

SMALL POTATOES IN OLIVE OIL

One evening my wife and I were eating freshly grilled sardines in Albufeira, in the south of Portugal, when the waiter brought us a plate of delightful boiled potatoes doused with olive oil. I adapted the recipe by adding olives for saltiness and color and cracking the potatoes open so they absorb some of the olive oil and coarse salt.

1½ pounds small potatoes, such as Yukon Gold or Red Bliss (about 16), scrubbed

½ teaspoon salt

¼ cup good extra-virgin olive oil

1 teaspoon fleur de sel or other coarse salt

12 kalamata olives, pitted and cut into ½-inch pieces

1½ tablespoons minced fresh chives

Put the potatoes in a saucepan and cover with water. Add the salt and bring the water to a boil, then reduce the heat to low and boil the potatoes gently for 25 to 30 minutes, until very tender.

Drain the potatoes and put in one layer in a serving dish.

Using a fork or the flat bottom of a measuring cup, press down gently on the potatoes to crack them open a little. Sprinkle with the oil, coarse salt, olives, and chives. Serve.

BAKER'S WIFE POTATOES

SERVES 8

"Baker's wife potatoes," or pommes de terre à la boulangère, *is the classic side dish for a roast leg of lamb. Mine are made with chicken stock and flavored with lots of onion; I add wine for a dash of acidity. It is important to cook the potatoes long enough: They should be soft and moist, but most of the liquid surrounding them should be evaporated or absorbed.*

The peeled potatoes can be set aside in water to cover, but don't slice them until just before assembling the dish. Soaking the slices in water would extract their starch, which is needed as a thickening agent to give the dish the proper texture.

2 pounds Yukon Gold potatoes

1 tablespoon peanut oil

4 cups thinly sliced onion (14 ounces)

6 large garlic cloves, thinly sliced (3 tablespoons)

3 cups homemade chicken stock or low-sodium canned chicken broth

1 teaspoon salt, or to taste

½ teaspoon freshly ground black pepper

½ cup dry white wine

3 bay leaves

2 fresh thyme sprigs

Preheat the oven to 375 degrees.

Peel the potatoes and cut them into ⅛-inch-thick slices.

Heat the oil in a large saucepan. When it is hot, add the onions and sauté them for 3 to 4 minutes. Add the remaining ingredients, including the potatoes, mixing gently, and bring to a boil. Transfer the mixture to an 8-cup gratin dish.

Bake for 50 minutes to 1 hour, until most of the moisture is absorbed and the potatoes are tender when pierced with a fork. Serve.

POTATOES RACHAEL RAY

Several years ago I made a potato dish called pommes fondantes *("melting potatoes") for a magazine article. I peeled and trimmed potatoes, cutting them into football shapes, and cooked them in a skillet in one layer with chicken stock and butter until the potatoes were done and the stock was practically gone. Then, using a large spoon, I pressed on the potatoes to crack them open without crushing them and cooked them for a few minutes longer. They absorbed the rest of the cooking liquid, browning beautifully in the butter.*

Not long ago, I was invited to appear on the Rachael Ray Show, *and, in my honor, she made those potatoes, incorporating a few changes of her own. She used small Yukon Gold potatoes and did not peel them. Since this made the dish easier to prepare and the result was just as good, I adjusted my own recipe accordingly.*

1¼ pounds baby yellow potatoes, such as Yukon Gold (about 20)

1½ cups homemade chicken stock or canned low-sodium chicken broth

2 tablespoons olive oil

¼ teaspoon salt (less if stock is salted)

2 tablespoons unsalted butter

2 tablespoons minced fresh chives

Remove and discard any eyes from the potatoes. Wash the potatoes and arrange them in one layer in a large skillet, preferably nonstick. Add the stock, oil, and salt and bring to a boil. Cover and cook gently for about 15 minutes, or until the potatoes are tender; there should be a little liquid left.

Using a metal measuring cup, press gently on each potato to crack it open, but do not mash the potatoes. Add the butter and cook the potatoes, uncovered, over medium heat, turning once, for about 3 minutes on each side, until all the liquid is gone and the potatoes are golden brown on both sides. Sprinkle with the chives and serve.

100 • JACQUES PÉPIN POULETS & LÉGUMES

FLUFFY MASHED POTATOES

SERVES 4

The mashed potatoes that my aunt from Valence made were better than any others. She told me once that the reason was the clove of unpeeled garlic she cooked with the potatoes. When she pushed the potatoes through a food mill or ricer, the garlic pulp contributed just a faint flavor. She always added butter to her mashed potatoes and made them with milk, never cream. Whisking the mixture makes it fluffy, creating what we call pommes mousseline *in French.*

Serve with Roast Split Chicken with Mustard Crust (page 13).

1 pound potatoes, preferably Yukon Gold or Red Bliss, peeled

1 large garlic clove, unpeeled

2½ tablespoons unsalted butter, softened

⅔ cup milk, heated in a microwave oven to warm, plus 2–3 more tablespoons milk if not serving the potatoes immediately

½ teaspoon salt

¼ teaspon freshly ground black pepper

Put the potatoes, garlic, and 3 cups water in a medium saucepan and bring to a boil over high heat. Reduce the heat and boil gently for about 25 minutes, or until the potatoes are fork-tender. Drain and push the potatoes through a food mill or ricer. (A food processor will make them gooey.) Add the butter and mix well with a wooden spoon until incorporated. Add about ⅓ cup of the milk and mix well with the spoon. Pour in the remaining ⅓ cup milk and add the salt and pepper. Using a whisk, whip the potatoes for 15 to 20 seconds, until they are fluffy and very smooth.

If the potatoes are not to be served immediately, smooth the top and pour 2 to 3 tablespoons milk on the potatoes to keep them moist. At serving time, stir the milk into the potatoes, reheat, and serve.

POTATO GRATIN WITH CREAM

~~~

I often serve boiled potatoes, with or without the skin, as an accompaniment to meat or fish. When I have some potatoes left over, I turn them into this sinfully rich potato gratin.

1 teaspoon unsalted butter, softened

About 1 pound boiled potatoes

¼ teaspoon freshly grated nutmeg

½ teaspoon salt

½ teaspoon freshly ground black pepper

1 cup heavy cream

¼ cup grated Parmesan cheese

Coat a 4- to 6-cup gratin dish with the butter. Preheat the oven to 400 degrees. If using cooked potatoes with skin, peel off the skin. Cut the potatoes into ¼-inch-thick slices. Arrange in the gratin dish. Sprinkle with the nutmeg, salt, and pepper and pour on the cream. Using a fork or spoon, press down on the top of the potato slices so they are level and wet with the cream.

Cover the top generously with the cheese and bake for 20 minutes, or until nicely browned, crusty, and hot. Serve.

BROILED MAPLE
SWEET POTATOES

SERVES 4

For this dish, I cook the sweet potatoes in a microwave oven while I heat up the broiler. Then I halve the potatoes, rub them with butter, top with maple syrup, and finish them under the broiler.

2 large sweet potatoes (2 pounds)

4 tablespoons (½ stick) unsalted butter, melted

4 teaspoons pure maple syrup

½ teaspoon salt

1 teaspoon freshly ground black pepper

Preheat the broiler. While it is heating, microwave the potatoes for 8 minutes. They should be cooked through. Split the potatoes lengthwise in half and score the flesh of each half with a knife, cutting a crisscross pattern about ½ inch deep. Brush the cut sides with half the butter and top with the maple syrup, salt, and pepper.

Arrange the potato halves cut side up on an aluminum foil–lined baking sheet and broil about 7 inches from the heat source for 4 minutes. Turn the potatoes over and broil for another 3 to 4 minutes.

Arrange the potatoes cut side up on a plate, brush with the remaining butter, and serve.

PUMPKIN GRATIN

The only way I ate pumpkin as a child was in a savory gratin, so the first time I had it in the United States—sweet, in a pie—I thought it was a mistake. I've come to love pumpkin pie, and I still enjoy pumpkin in the gratin of my youth. The combination of Swiss cheese, eggs, and cream comes together into something like a smooth and creamy soufflé, capturing the flavors of fall. Canned pumpkin speeds things up.

1 (15.5-ounce) can 100% pure pumpkin puree (not pumpkin pie filling)

3 large eggs

1 cup heavy cream

¾ cup grated Swiss cheese

¾ teaspoon salt

½ teaspoon freshly ground black pepper

1 teaspoon unsalted butter

1 tablespoon grated Parmesan cheese

Preheat the oven to 350 degrees. Spoon the pumpkin puree into a food processor and add the eggs, cream, cheese, salt, and pepper. Process for 10 to 15 seconds to combine.

Coat a 6-cup gratin dish with the butter. Fill the dish with the pumpkin mixture. Sprinkle the Parmesan cheese on top and bake for 35 to 45 minutes, until set and lightly browned on top. Serve.

VELVET SPINACH

This puree, or "velvet," is made with tender baby spinach, but any fresh spinach will work. A little butter, salt, and pepper are the only enhancements in this preparation, which concentrates the beautiful green color and the pure taste of the fresh spinach.

1 pound baby spinach

3 tablespoons unsalted butter

¾ teaspoon salt

¾ teaspoon freshly ground black pepper

Bring 3 cups water to a boil in a medium saucepan. Add the spinach and push it down into the water to wilt it. Bring the water back to a boil and boil the spinach, uncovered, for about 1 minute.

Drain the spinach in a colander, reserving a little of the cooking water, and transfer to a blender. Add the butter, salt, and pepper and blend until the spinach is finely pureed. If the mixture is too thick to process properly, add 1 or 2 tablespoons of the reserved cooking water and process until smooth. Serve.

CLASSIC RATATOUILLE

Ratatouille is the epitome of Provençal vegetable stews. The vegetables are sautéed individually in oil before being stewed, so they keep their shape and texture. If you prefer, though, you can put all the cubed vegetables into a casserole and top with the seasonings and water. Ratatouille is excellent reheated and it is superb cold as an hors d'oeuvre, topped with small black olives and olive oil.

About ½ cup olive oil

1 eggplant (1¼ pounds), trimmed but not peeled and cut into 1-inch cubes (about 4 cups)

3 medium zucchini (about 1¼ pounds), trimmed and cut into 1-inch cubes (about 3 cups)

12 ounces onions, diced (1-inch)

1 pound green bell peppers (2–3), cored, seeded, and diced (1-inch) (about 3 cups)

4–5 ripe tomatoes, peeled, halved, seeded, and coarsely cubed (about 4 cups)

5–6 garlic cloves, crushed and very finely chopped (about 1 tablespoon)

½ cup water

2 teaspoons salt

½ teaspoon freshly ground black pepper

Heat ¼ cup of the oil in one or, better, two large skillets. First sauté the eggplant cubes until browned, about 8 minutes; remove with a slotted spoon and transfer to a large heavy flameproof casserole. (The eggplant will absorb more oil while cooking than the other vegetables.) Then sauté the zucchini cubes until browned, about 8 minutes. Transfer to the casserole. Add about ¼ cup more oil to the pan and sauté the onions and peppers together for about 6 minutes. Add them to the casserole.

Add the tomatoes, garlic, water, salt, and pepper to the casserole and bring to a boil over medium heat. Reduce the heat to low, cover, and cook for 1 hour.

Remove the cover, increase the heat to medium, and cook for another 20 minutes to reduce the liquid; stir once in a while to prevent scorching. Let the ratatouille rest for at least 30 minutes before serving.

🍂 How to Peel and Seed Tomatoes

Dip the tomatoes briefly in boiling water or hold them over the flame of a gas stove, then peel them with a knife; the skin should slide off easily. Alternatively, peel the tomatoes with a sharp vegetable peeler. To seed the tomatoes, cut them crosswise in half and squeeze the seeds out. The seeds, juice, and skin can be frozen for use in stock.

CARAMELIZED TOMATOES PROVENÇAL

SERVES 4

There are many versions of tomatoes Provençal, in which tomatoes are baked with parsley, garlic, and olive oil. I use plum (Roma) tomatoes, which stay quite firm and meaty even when fully ripe. I get the pan quite hot before I add the oiled tomato halves. The tomatoes caramelize, but they can often stick to the pan: The secret is to leave them off the heat for 5 to 10 minutes after browning so they soften, release some of their liquid, and release from the pan.

8 firm plum tomatoes (about 2 pounds)

4 tablespoons olive oil

½ teaspoon salt

½ teaspoon freshly ground black pepper

1¼ cups diced (¼-inch) stale baguette

¼ cup coarsely chopped fresh parsley

1 tablespoon coarsely chopped garlic

2 tablespoons grated Gruyère or Emmenthaler cheese

Preheat the oven to 400 degrees.

Cut the tomatoes lengthwise in half. Spread 2 tablespoons of the oil in a gratin dish that can accommodate all the tomatoes and place them cut side down in the oil. Heat a heavy saucepan (not nonstick) over high heat for at least 5 minutes, until it is very hot. Add the oiled tomato halves, cut side down, in one layer and cook for about 5 minutes to caramelize the cut sides of the tomatoes. Turn the heat off and let the tomatoes stand for 5 to 10 minutes. They will release some juices and so will not stick to the pan anymore. Return the tomato halves to the gratin dish, arranging them browned side up. Sprinkle with the salt and pepper. Mix the bread pieces with the parsley, garlic, cheese, and the remaining 2 tablespoons oil. Spread on top of the tomato halves. (This can be done hours ahead.)

Shortly before serving time, place the tomatoes in the center of the oven and cook for 20 to 25 minutes, until hot, bubbling, and browned on top. Serve.

SLICED TOMATO GRATIN

SERVES 4

Thick slices of ripe tomato are baked with a topping of diced bread and seasonings in this gratin. Success depends on using the highest-quality ingredients.

2 pounds large ripe tomatoes

3 tablespoons olive oil

2 cups diced (½-inch) baguette or country bread

⅔ cup sliced shallots

⅓ cup sliced garlic

1½ teaspoons fresh thyme leaves

½ teaspoon salt

½ teaspoon freshly ground black pepper

Preheat the oven to 425 degrees.

Cut the tomatoes into ½-inch slices and arrange the slices in a 6- to 8-cup gratin dish. Sprinkle with 2 tablespoons of the oil.

Combine the bread, shallots, garlic, thyme, and the remaining 1 tablespoon oil in a bowl and mix well. Sprinkle the salt and pepper on the tomatoes and top with the bread mixture. Bake for about 25 minutes, until the tomatoes are browned on top and cooked. Serve.

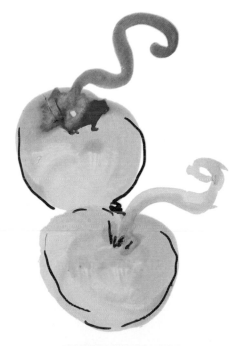

STUFFED TOMATOES

Any good home cook in France has her own special recipe for stuffed tomatoes. My mother, aunt, cousins, and niece all made their versions when the season yielded large and inexpensive tomatoes. For mine, I combine mushrooms and zucchini with meat, onions, garlic, and hot pepper to a make a flavorful and moist stuffing. I use a mixture of hot Italian pork sausage and ground beef. I cut a good ¾-inch slice from the stem end of each tomato and then hollow out the tomatoes. These top slices and the insides of the tomatoes are pureed in a food processor to become the sauce. If you have extra tomato puree, it can be used for soup, pasta, or even drinks.

6 large not-too-ripe tomatoes (about 10 ounces each; 3½ pounds total)

1¼ teaspoons salt

2 tablespoons olive oil

2 tablespoons potato starch dissolved in 2 tablespoons water

5 ounces baby bella or cremini mushrooms, washed, cubed, and coarsely chopped in a food processor (about 2 cups)

2 small firm zucchini (8 ounces total), cubed and coarsely chopped in the food processor (about 2 cups)

½ cup chopped onion

1 tablespoon chopped garlic

Preheat the oven to 400 degrees.

Remove the stems of the tomatoes, if any, and reserve for decoration. Cut a thick slice (about ¾ inch) from the stem end of each tomato. Using a sharp spoon (a metal measuring spoon is good), hollow out each tomato to make a receptacle, leaving a ½- to ¾-inch-thick shell.

Process the slices and insides of the tomatoes in a food processor. (You should have about 3 cups; if you have more, keep the excess for a soup or sauce.) Transfer to a bowl, add ½ teaspoon of the salt, the olive oil, and dissolved potato starch, and mix well with a whisk.

Transfer the mixture to a saucepan, bring to a boil, and cook, stirring occasionally. The sauce will thicken as it comes to a boil. Strain through a food mill or sieve. Set aside.

½ cup chopped fresh parsley
or minced chives, plus
2 tablespoons for garnish

2 teaspoons chopped jalapeño
pepper

½ teaspoon freshly ground
black pepper

8 ounces ground beef

8 ounces hot Italian sausage
patties, bulk Italian sausage, or
links, casings removed

Combine the mushrooms, zucchini, onion, garlic, parsley or chives, jalapeño pepper, the remaining ¾ teaspoon salt, the pepper, ground beef, and sausage in a bowl and mix well with your hands. Arrange the tomato receptacles side by side, hollow side up, in a large gratin dish and fill with the stuffing mix (about 1 cup per tomato). Place the stems, if you have them, on top for decoration. Pour the sauce around and over the tomatoes.

Bake the tomatoes for 1 hour. Serve with some of the sauce and a sprinkling of the remaining 2 tablespoons parsley or chives.

INDEX

A

Anchoïade, Cabbage, 59
Anchovies
    Baby Artichokes with, 69
    Cabbage Anchoïade, 59
    Chicken Mayonnaise, 34
    Chicken Tonnato, 35–36
    Tapenade, 37
Apples
    Roast Stuffed Cornish Hens, 60–61
    Sweet-and-Spicy Curried Chicken, 52–53
Artichoke(s)
    Baby, with Anchovies, 69
    Hearts and Peas, 68
    Hearts with Tarragon and Mushrooms, 66
    preparing and cooking, 67
Arugula
    Chicken Tonnato, 35–36
Asparagus
    in Mustard Sauce, 72
    Topped with Bread Crumbs and Eggs, 70–71
    trimming, 72

B

Bacon and Brussels Sprouts, Fricassee of, 74
Bananas
    Sweet-and-Spicy Curried Chicken, 52–53
Basil, Peas with, 93
Beans. *See* Haricots Verts
Beef
    Stuffed Tomatoes, 112–13
Bouillabaisse, Chicken, 44–45

Bread Crumbs
    Baked Chicken with Herb Crumbs, 14–15
    Cauliflower à la Polonaise, 80–81
    and Eggs, Asparagus Topped with, 70–71
Bread toasts
    Croutons, 25–26
    Wild Mushroom Toasts, 96
Broccoli, Piquant Steamed, with Lemon Sauce, 73
Brown Sauce, Basic, 57
Brussels Sprouts and Bacon, Fricassee of, 74
Bulgur
    Roast Stuffed Cornish Hens, 60–61

C

Cabbage Anchoïade, 59
Capers
    Chicken Mayonnaise, 34
    Chicken Tonnato, 35–36
    Chicken with Saffron Rice, 51
    Glazed Carrots with Olives, 75
    Tapenade, 37
Carrots
    Chicken Jardinière, 48–49
    with Chives, 77
    Glazed, with Olives, 75
    Normandy Chicken Fricassee, 32–33
Cauliflower
    à la Polonaise, 80–81
    au Gratin, 78
    Sauté à Cru, 79

Cheese
    Caramelized Tomatoes Provençal, 110
    Cauliflower au Gratin, 78
    Eggplant and Tomato Gratin, 88
    Potato Gratin with Cream, 102
    Pumpkin Gratin, 105
    Chervil Mousse, Chicken Breasts with, 22–23
Chicken
    African-Style, with Couscous, 28–29
    Baked, with Herb Crumbs, 14–15
    Bouillabaisse, 44–45
    Breasts, Spicy, 20
    Breasts with Chervil Mousse, 22–23
    Breasts with Garlic and Parsley, 21
    Chasseur, 46–47
    with Cognac Sauce, 16–17
    Curried, Sweet-and-Spicy, 52–53
    Diable, 30–31
    Fricassee, Normandy, 32–33
    Grilled, with Cabbage Anchoïade, 58–59
    Grilled, with Herb Sauce, 56
    Grilled, with Tarragon Butter, 55
    Jardinière, 48–49
    Mayonnaise, 34
    Peking-Style, 18–19
    Poulet à la Crème, 41
    Quick Coq au Vin, 24–26
    removing wishbone from, 19
    and Rice with Cumin and Cilantro, 39
    Roast, 10–11
    Roast Split, with Mustard Crust, 13
    with Saffron Rice, 51
    Suprêmes with Tapenade and Mushroom Sauce,
        37–38
    Tenders, Grilled, with Chimichurri, 54

    Thighs, Crusty, with Mushroom Sauce, 42–43
    Tonnato, 35–36
    trussing, 19
Chimichurri Sauce, 54
Chives
    Carrots with, 77
    Cauliflower Sauté à Cru, 79
Cilantro
    Chimichurri Sauce, 54
    and Cumin, Chicken and Rice with, 39
    Eggplant Chinois, 85
Cognac
    Chicken Breasts with Chervil Mousse, 22–23
    Sauce, Chicken with, 16–17
Corn
    Pancakes, Crispy, 83
    and Shallots with Sun-Dried Tomatoes, 82
Cornish Hens
    boning, technique for, 62
    Roast Stuffed, 60–61
Couscous, Chicken African-Style with, 28–29
Croutons, 25–26
Cucumbers in Cream, 84
Cumin and Cilantro, Chicken and Rice with, 39
Curried Chicken, Sweet-and-Spicy, 52–53

D

Dressing, Mustard and Cream, 91

E

Eggplant
    Chinois, 85
    Classic Ratatouille, 108
    Fans, Fried, 86–87
    and Tomato Gratin, 88

Eggs
  and Bread Crumbs, Asparagus Topped with,
    70–71
  Cauliflower à la Polonaise, 80–81
  Chicken Mayonnaise, 34
Endive, Braised, 89

F

Fennel and Peas with Lardons, 95
Fish. *See* Anchovies; Tuna

G

Garlic
  Cabbage Anchoïade, 59
  Cauliflower Sauté à Cru, 79
  Chicken and Rice with Cumin and Cilantro, 39
  Eggplant Chinois, 85
  and Parsley, Chicken Breasts with, 21
  and Parsley, Sautéed Potatoes with, 97
  Rouille, 44–45
  Sliced Tomatoes Gratin, 111
Ginger
  Chicken African-Style with Couscous, 28–29
  Chicken and Rice with Cumin and Cilantro, 39
  Eggplant Chinois, 85

H

Haricots Verts
  Green Beans with Mustard and Cream Dressing,
    91
  and Shallots, Sautéed, 90
Herb(s). *See also specific herbs*
  Crumbs, Baked Chicken with, 14–15
  Sauce, Grilled Chicken with, 56

L

Lardons, Peas and Fennel with, 95
Leeks with Tomatoes and Olive Oil, 92
Lemon(s)
  Grilled Chicken with Cabbage Anchoïade, 58–59
  Sauce, Piquant Steamed Broccoli with, 73
Lettuce
  Chicken Mayonnaise, 34
  Peas à la Française, 94

M

Maple Sweet Potatoes, Broiled, 104
Mayonnaise, Chicken, 34
Mousse, Chervil, Chicken Breasts with, 22–23
Mushroom(s)
  Chicken Chasseur, 46–47
  Chicken Jardinière, 48–49
  Peking-Style Chicken, 18–19
  Poulet à la Crème, 41
  Quick Coq au Vin, 24–26
  Sauce, Crusty Chicken Thighs with, 42–43
  Sauce and Tapenade, Chicken Suprêmes with,
    37–38
  Stuffed Tomatoes, 112–13
  and Tarragon, Artichoke Hearts with, 66
  Wild, Toasts, 96
Mustard
  and Cream Dressing, Green Beans with, 91
  Crust, Roast Split Chicken with, 13
  Sauce, Asparagus in, 72

O

Olives
  Chicken with Saffron Rice, 51

Glazed Carrots with, 75
Small Potatoes in Olive Oil, 98
Tapenade, 37
Onions
  Baker's Wife Potatoes, 99
  Chicken Jardinière, 48–49
  Peas à la Française, 94
  Quick Coq au Vin, 24–26
Oregano
  Chimichurri Sauce, 54
  Grilled Chicken with Cabbage Anchoïade, 58–59

P

Pancakes, Crispy Corn, 83
Parsley
  and Garlic, Chicken Breasts with, 21
  and Garlic, Sautéed Potatoes with, 97
Peas
  à la Française, 94
  Artichoke Hearts and, 68
  with Basil, 93
  Chicken Jardinière, 48–49
  and Fennel with Lardons, 95
  Normandy Chicken Fricassee, 32–33
Peppers
  Cabbage Anchoïade, 59
  Classic Ratatouille, 108
Pork. See Lardons; Sausages
Potato(es)
  Baker's Wife, 99
  Chicken Bouillabaisse, 44–45
  Chicken Jardinière, 48–49
  Gratin with Cream, 102
  Mashed, Fluffy, 101
  Rachael Ray, 100

Sautéed, with Parsley and Garlic, 97
Small, in Olive Oil, 98
Sweet, Broiled Maple, 104
Poultry. See also Chicken
  Roast Stuffed Cornish Hens, 60–61
  small, boning, technique for, 62
Pumpkin Gratin, 105

R

Ratatouille, Classic, 108
Rice
  Chicken and, with Cumin and Cilantro, 39
  Saffron, Chicken with, 51
Rouille, 44–45

S

Saffron
  Chicken Bouillabaisse, 44–45
  Rice, Chicken with, 51
Sauces
  Basic Brown, 57
  Chimichurri, 54
  Lemon, 73
  Mustard, 72
Sausages
  Chicken Bouillabaisse, 44–45
  Stuffed Tomatoes, 112–13
Shallots
  and Corn with Sun-Dried Tomatoes, 82
  and Haricots Verts, Sautéed, 90
  Sliced Tomatoes Gratin, 111
Spinach, Velvet, 107
Squash. See Pumpkin; Zucchini
Sweet Potatoes, Broiled Maple, 104

T

Tapenade, 37
Tarragon
    Butter, Grilled Chicken with, 55
    and Mushrooms, Artichoke Hearts with, 66
Tomato(es)
    Caramelized, Provençal, 110
    Chicken and Rice with Cumin and Cilantro, 39
    Chicken Bouillabaisse, 44–45
    Chicken Chasseur, 46–47
    Chicken Diable, 30–31
    Chicken Mayonnaise, 34
    Chicken with Saffron Rice, 51
    Classic Ratatouille, 108
    and Eggplant Gratin, 88
    and Olive Oil, Leeks with, 92
    peeling and seeding, 109
    Sliced, Gratin, 111
Stuffed, 112–13
    Sun-Dried, Corn and Shallots with, 82
Tuna
    Chicken Tonnato, 35–36

Z

Zucchini
    Classic Ratatouille, 108
    Stuffed Tomatoes, 112–13